# How To Hike Dogs At Our National Parks - Even When They're Not Allowed On The Trail

DOUG GELBERT

*illustrations by*

ANDREW CHESWORTH

CRUDEN BAY BOOKS

**There is always a new trail to look forward to...**

Cruden Bay Books
www.hikewithyourdog.com
crudbay@mac.com

International Standard Book Number  978-1-935771-28-9

*"Dogs are our link to paradise...to sit with a dog on a hillside on a glorious afternoon is to be back in Eden, where doing nothing was not boring - it was peace."*
*- Milan Kundera*

# Ahead On The Trail

# Introduction

Dogs and parks. Wed two of our favorite things together and you have the makings of a perfect day, right? Except at America's national parks. Save for a few exceptions, dogs are never allowed on national park trails and rarely permitted beyond a campground or picnic area.

There is an old saying that goes, "Start explaining and you've lost the argument." The National Park Service goes to great lengths to explain their reasons for banning dogs outside of vehicles. Dogs endanger wildlife. Dogs interfere with people's enjoyment of the park. Dogs ruin the pristine environment. Dogs can introduce diseases that could decimate wild populations. Some parks cite the fact that just the scent of dogs will make prey animals frantic (at least that will keep the jittery critters out of campgrounds and picnics where apparently their well-being is not as big a concern).

Some park officials go so far as to imply that they are doing dog owners a favor by keeping dogs out of the woods since they may become prey themselves. One park's regulations read thusly: "*There is a strong possibility that your pet could become prey for a bear, coyote, owl, or other predator.*" What is a "strong possibility?" Better than 50%? 20%? Any talk of the probability of a leashed dog on a trail being eaten by a wild animal that goes beyond "vanishingly small probability" is absurd.

Tellingly, the national parks in Canada - which also receive millions of visitors each year and also protect wildlife - allow dogs on their trails almost without exception. And in the United States the prohibition against dogs on national park trails is not a universal edict. Individual parks are allowed to make their own rules regarding dogs. A handful have decided to allow dogs on the trails, the chance of their becoming some other animal's dinner be damned. Some have even become more lenient in recent years. Petrified Forest National Park used to allow dogs only on a few nature trails. Now the park declares: *"Petrified Forest is a very pet friendly national park! Please take your furry friends on trails, even backpacking in the wilderness area."*

This is not a book about whether rules regarding dogs in national parks are right or wrong. It is about how dog owners - given the current restrictive playing field - can experience our national parks, take along their best trail companions, and still have their dream vacation. For each park, if dogs are not allowed on the trails, a nearby substitute is identified and described (dogs are usually welcome in national forests, for example. The burden on people and wildlife caused by dogs and a patronizing concern for a dog's well-being apparently cause less government worry in those woods). Only those national parks which can be reached by automobile are included.

**So with that in mind, grab a leash and hit the trail!**

## The Park

Samuel Champlain guided a French expedition that landed here on September 5, 1604. In claiming the land for France, Champlain, noting the bare, rocky mountain humps, called his discovery "Isles des Monts Desert." In the Gilded Age of the end of the 19th century tycoons like the Rockefellers, Astors, Fords, and Vanderbilts all built lavish summer estates on Mount Desert Island. One, George B. Dorr, devoted 43 years and much of his family fortune to preserving the island and gave 6,000 acres to the federal government for safekeeping. In 1919 Woodrow Wilson made Acadia, originally named Lafayette, the first national park east of the Mississippi River.

**WHERE/WHEN**

Maine/1919

**OFFICIAL POLICY REGARDING DOGS**

There are 100 miles of hiking trails and 45 miles of carriage roads in the park where dogs are permitted; Blackwoods and Seawall Campgrounds allow pets.

## What Your Dog Will Miss

Almost nothing! Acadia National Park is one of the crown jewels in the National Park Service and dogs will not bark in dissent. Only a handful of park trails are off-limits to dogs and several of these, such as the celebrated *Precipice Trail* up the east side of Champlain Mountain, involve insurmountable ladders or vertical climbs anyway.

More than 45 miles of carriage roads ripple across Mount Desert Island, constructed by park patron John D. Rockefeller, Jr. who was no great fan of the newfangled horseless carriage. The rustic broken stone roads were hand-built between 1913 and 1940 and are the best examples of the construction technique still in use in America. In addition to the irregularly spaced granite slab guardrails known colloquially as "Rockefeller's Teeth," there are 16 stone-faced bridges - each unique in design.

Much of your dog's hiking will take place around more than a dozen small mountain peaks that were blazed by early settlers and later incorporated into a master trail plan for the island that began in 1891. The tallest is the 1,530-foot Cadillac Mountain that is the highest point on the Atlantic Ocean north of Rio de Janeiro, Brazil. Sunrise hikes here will be the

*Hiking past Bubble Rock at Acadia National Park.*

first illuminated in the United States. The *Jordan Pond Nature Trail* is a mile-long loop leading to views of glacial mountains reflecting in the pond waters. The rounded mountains framing the pond, known as the Bubbles, can be climbed on short trails.

Some of the most rewarding canine hiking in Acadia takes place on the headlands overlooking the ocean. The *Great Head Trail* loops across Sand Beach and most people go right at the head of the loop. But going left into the maritime forest saves the spectacular coastal views until the end. In the western reaches of the park across Somes Sound - America's only fjord - expect to find far fewer paw prints on the trail.

------------------------------------------------------------

# Nearby Places to Hike With Your Dog

Bar Harbor is the main town on Mount Desert Island, squeezed between Acadia National Park and the Atlantic Ocean. In the 1800s wealthy vacationers began claiming homesites on the water but private

landowners have provided a sliver of land for the public to enjoy the for over 100 years. The curvilinear Shore Path is a gravel walkway, starting at the Town Pier, absolutely level and ideal for strolling. When the waves are gentle there are numerous spots for your dog to drop down and play in the tidal pools of Frenchman Bay.

*The town gazebo is the rendezvous point for your dog's explorations of Bar Harbor.*

# ARCHES NATIONAL PARK

## The Park

Some 300 million years ago a great sea covered this slice of Utah setting the stage for one of the planet's greatest concentration of natural arches after it evaporated. As the salt bed settled and shifted domes of sandstone were uplifted that have since eroded into a collection of over 2,000 arches. It takes a three-foot opening to be called an arch but Arches National Park boasts some salmon-colored Entrada Sandstone and buff-colored Navajo Sandstone bridges that stretch the length of a football field. The Arches have been a national monument since the 1920s with shifting boundaries over the years bringing new arches under protection. One of President Lyndon Johnson's final acts in office was to substantially increase the Arches before it ultimately became a national park.

**WHERE/WHEN**

Utah/1971

**OFFICIAL POLICY REGARDING DOGS**

Dogs are allowed only on park roads and in parking lots. Dogs are not allowed on trails or in the backcountry. Dogs can stay in Devil's Garden Campground, the only campground in the park.

## What Your Dog Will Miss

Most of the trails in Arches National Park are short foot paths that lead from the parking lots to featured arches like the Windows, Landscape Arch and the wondrously situated Delicate Arch the symbol of Utah's license plate). If you are visiting the park in cooler weather you can see many of these arches while your dog waits in the car. Hardier day hikes await in the Devils Garden Area.

*Taking the final steps to Wilson's Arch.*

# Nearby Places to Hike With Your Dog

So how can my dog get up close and personal with a sculpted rock arch outside the national park? Well, how about a hike to the world's fifth longest natural arch and America's third longest? Just six miles to the east of the entrance to Arches National Park, on the opposite side of the town of Moab and up Scenic Route 128, is the trailhead for Negro Bill Canyon. Back in the 1870s William Granstaff, the product of several races, ran cattle in the canyon while he split up possession of the Spanish Valley with his erstwhile partner, a French-Canadian trapper known only as "Frenchie." Granstaff high-tailed out of the territory in 1881 when the law accused him of illegally selling liquor to local Indians. All he left behind was his name.

A little more than two miles up into the canyon, pressed back against rock wall, is multi-hued Morning Glory Natural Bridge that stretches 243 feet across a pool of water. The packed-sand *Negro Bill Canyon Trail* crosses a shallow-flowing stream many times on its journey up the canyon and you may need your dog's nose to stay on course from time to time in the richly vegetated canyon. Recent rains can transform the water hole under the arch into an ideal doggie swimming pool.

In this part of Utah you can find arches that are not even in protected lands, just hanging out on the roadside. About 24 miles south of Moab on the east side of Route 191 stands Wilson Arch, named for an early pioneer who grubstaked a cabin near here. You can just park by the side of the road and scramble up the rock face with your dog to stand under the 46-foot high sandstone arch.

*Making the final approach to the Morning Glory Natural Bridge.*

## The Park

Badlands get their name not from being good places for outlaws to hide out in but from the prospect of dispirited pioneers having to maneuver wagons through the eroded clay pinnacles and coulees. In addition to these awe-inspiring rock formations the national park protects a vibrant mixed-grass prairie and some of the world's richest fossil beds. Where bison, prairie dogs, bighorn sheep and America's most endangered mammal, the black-footed ferret, live today saber-toothed cats and rhino once patrolled.

**WHERE/WHEN**
South Dakota/1978

**OFFICIAL POLICY REGARDING DOGS**
Dogs are prohibited from hiking trails and back-country areas, including the Badlands Wilderness Area. Dogs can stay in the campgrounds and hike anywhere that is open to motor vehicles.

## What Your Dog Will Miss

The backbone of the park is the Badlands Loop Road with its series of overlooks of the alien landscape. Hiking outside of the wilderness area is not a major feature of Badlands National Park, featuring mostly short interpretive trails. So your dog will not miss a whole lot.

-------------------------------------------------------------

# Nearby Places to Hike With Your Dog

Nothing nearby can exactly replicate the otherworldly experience of the Badlands but there is plenty of room for your dog to roam just next door in the Buffalo Gap National Grassland. The national grassland is no slouch when it comes to spectacular geological formations and is a wonderland for rockhounding. There is only one modest recreation area with a developed trail through the wispy grass prairie; wooden posts lead the way. Two-track dirt jeep roads also penetrate into land of badland formations and prairie dogs, some of which will lead you to the shadow of the Minuteman Missile National Historic Site.

Your dog can experience some of America's most striking badlands formations just across the state line in the Nebraska panhandle at the Oglala National Grassland. To give your dog a chance to explore these unique lands of sculpted rock, head south from the Dakotas to the lesser-known badlands of Toadstool Geologic Park where the relentless tag-team of water and wind have carved fanciful rock designs into the stark hills.

*In the American badlands wooden posts do the duty of wayfinding.*

The "toadstools" form when underlying soft clay stone erodes faster than the hard sandstone that caps it. A marked, mile-long interpretive loop leads you on an educational adventure where your dog is welcome on the hard rock trail but can also explore off the path for close-up looks in the gullies at fossil bone fragments that lace the rocks and 30-million year-old footprints preserved in the stone. For extended hikes, Toadstool Park connects to the world-renowned Hudson-Meng Bison Boneyard via a three-mile trail. This archeological marvel seeks to unravel the mystery of how over 600 bison died nearly 10,000 years ago in an area about the size of a football stadium. Human predation is the leading suspect.

*Exploring the wonders of Toadstool Geologic Park in the badlands of the Nebraska Panhandle.*

## The Park

The Rio Grande River establishes an international border of over 1,000 miles between the United States and Mexico and Big Bend National Park includes 118 miles of that boundary. This is the largest chunk of protected Chihuahuan Desert in the United States - the park is larger than the entire state of Rhode Island. More than 450 bird species are known to take refuge in the remote mountains and rugged canyons of Big Bend.

## What Your Dog Will Miss

Big Bend offers some 200 miles of hiking trails from hardscrabble desert treks to twenty miles of exploration in the Chisos Mountains that rise to 7,832 feet in elevation atop Emory Peak. Poking in and out of the canyons of the Rio Grande in a canoe will be left to non-dog owners as well.

**WHERE/WHEN**
Texas/1944

**OFFICIAL POLICY REGARDING DOGS**
Dogs are not allowed on trails, off roads, or on the Rio Grande River. Your dog can go only where your car can go.

The Ross Maxwell Scenic Drive is the marquee touring road in Big Bend but your dog will have to sit out the short walks to the historic ranch sites on the route and the picturesque Santa Elena Canyon.

--------------------------------------------------------------

# Nearby Places to Hike With Your Dog

Texas may be the most massive of the Lower 48 states but scarcely three percent of the land is publicly owned. Big Bend represents the largest expanse of roadless public lands in the Lone Star State and neighboring Big Bend Ranch State Park is not welcoming to dogs either. On the state park lands dogs are not permitted more than 400 yards from a campsite or a designated road although your best trail companion can trot on the *Closed Canyon Trail* and the *Hoodoos Trail* along Route 170 that hugs the international border near the Rio Grande River.

So when you bring your dog to Big Bend it is essentially the national park or nothing. Luckily your dog need not be trapped in the car during your visit. While there are over 100 miles of paved roads for touring there are even more miles of dirt roads criss-crossing the 800,000 acres that can double as hiking trails for dogs. High-clearance vehicles can access the unimproved "Primitive Roads" that run through canyons and dry washes. While these hikes on dirt roads with your dog will not show

*Common sights for dogs hiking in West Texas.*

up as highlights in the park brochure they can lead to the remains of ancient settlements and centuries-old cemeteries. Some of these axle-challenging wagon trails to seek out include the Old Ore Road north of the Rio Grande Village, Old Maverick Road off the Ross Maxwell Scenic Drive and the Boquillas Canyon Road.

# BLACK CANYON OF THE GUNNISON NATIONAL PARK

## The Park

Although largely unknown, no other canyon in North America combines the narrow opening, sheer walls, and startling depths offered by the Black Canyon of the Gunnison. The uplifted hard rock is being gouged by an energetic river dropping an average of 96 feet per mile in the park; at its narrowest the canyon walls are a mere 40 feet apart. The gorge earns its intimidating name by experiencing scarcely a half hour of sunlight a day deep inside its walls.

## What Your Dog Will Miss

Not very much if you are not planning any adventurous below-the-rim hiking on steep, unmaintained trails or running the river.

**WHERE/WHEN**
Colorado/1999

**OFFICIAL POLICY REGARDING DOGS**
Dogs are not allowed on the inner canyon trails or in the wilderness areas.

------------------------------------------------------------

# Nearby Places to Hike With Your Dog

Visitors absorb the Black Canyon from short nature trails that lead to the edges of the rocky cliffs that plunge a half-mile down to the Gunnison River and your dog can hike them all. These include the *Rim Rock Trail* and the *Cedar Point Nature Trail* on the south rim and the the *Chasm View Nature Trail* on the north rim. This is flat, easy-going canine hiking but there is little in the way of shade among the desert-like scrub vegetation so take precautions on hot summer scorchers.

Three dams downstream from the national park have tamed the Gunnison River. The first was the Blue Mesa Dam and when it was completed in 1945 the reservoir it created became the largest body of water in Colorado. Each of the three dams supports a recreation area that has been cobbled into the Curecanti National Recreation Area, administered by the National Park Service.

Dogs are allowed on all the park trails, several of which deliver the same experience of sheer canyon walls as the neighboring national park. The sporty *Mesa Creek Trail* at Crystal Reservoir is one of those. The unique geology of the Black Canyon is interpreted along the *Dillon Pinnacles Trail* at Blue Mesa

*You take what shade you can find on the rim of Black Canyon.*

Reservoir which are eroded volcanic souvenirs of the Precambrian age 1.7 billion years ago. The Curecanti Needle, a 700-foot triangular rock rising from the canyon floor, is the star at Morrow Point Reservoir.

Just north of the Black Canyon of the Gunnison National Park is Grand Mesa, the largest flattop mountain in the world. The top destination here is the *Crag Crest National Recreation Trail*, a 10-mile circle trail that climbs to over 11,000 feet on a boulder-strewn crest affording great perches for views of alpine lakes. The lower elevations drop among quaking aspen and Englemann spruce for lively meadow walks and refreshing canine swimming holes.

*Down in the Black Canyon is one place your dog won't be hiking.*

# BRYCE CANYON NATIONAL PARK

## The Park

"Helluva place to lose a cow." That is what homesteader Ebenezer Bryce said when he brought his wife to run cattle in the Paria Valley in the 1870s. The eastern edge of the Paunsaugunt Plateau had eroded into a series of horseshoe-shaped amphitheaters filled with spires and windows and limestone formations in colors that Crayola would be hard pressed to duplicate with its largest box of crayons. The dark green Ponderosa pines accent the vibrant colors in the park even more dramatically.

## What Your Dog Will Miss

Unfortunately some of the most unforgettable hiking in the National Park System is off-limits to your dog. The *Under-the-Rim Trail*, the *Peek-A-Boo Trail* and others that wind through the stunning pink Claron limestone spires known as "hoodoos" do not permit dogs.

**WHERE/WHEN**
Utah/1928

**OFFICIAL POLICY REGARDING DOGS**
Dogs are allowed only in campgrounds, parking lots and paved roads. You can also walk your dog along the short trail near Bryce Canyon Lodge between Sunset Point and Sunrise Point; it is also paved.

Dogs also can not trot the *Bristlecone Loop* among the oldest living trees on earth, even if the Bristlecones in Bryce are comparable arboreal children at only 1,600 years young compared to their ancient cousins found in California and Nevada.

# Nearby Places to Hike With Your Dog

The Red Canyon has been called the "most photographed place in Utah," which is quite a boast when Bryce Canyon is a mere 13 miles down the road. But Red Canyon backs up its tough talk with Ponderosa pine trees and sculpted rock formations rising out of brilliant red soil.

*Bryce Canyon is not the only place in the Utah desert to enjoy a multi-chromatic canine hike.*

Their numbers are not as intense as in the national park but there are the same pinnacles, hoodoos and spires to be seen along the *Pink Ledges Trail* and the *Photo Trail* and the *Tunnel Trail*. The Red Canyon Trail System through the valley that is cut into the side of the Paunsaugunt Plateau also has longer explorations that accommodate bicycles, horses and ATVs.

On assignment for the National Geographic Society in 1949 explorers were so entranced by the Utah desert that they named one basin filled with sedimentary rock pipes and geysers after the Kodak film they were using to capture the explosion of colors - Kodachrome Basin. In 1962 when the area became a state park it was called Kodachrome Basin State Park. The park's splendors unfurl along a series of hard-scrabble trails through the box canyons and rock formations that can be completed in less than an hour. The park star, the *Panorama Trail*, is pocked with side trail adventures that push its distance out to almost twice its 2.9-mile length. With dozens of sand pipes soaring as high as 170 feet Kodachrome Basin State Park will have your dog thinking it is a hike over the hills in the more renowned Bryce Canyon.

# CANYONLANDS NATIONAL PARK

## The Park

Canyonlands is about as primitive as the national park system gets and that is just referencing the accessible Islands in the Sky and Needles districts. A third district, The Maze, is so remote visitors are advised to be "prepared for self-sufficiency and the proper equipment or gear for self-rescue." The Islands in the Sky is characterized by canyons carved into the Colorado Plateau by the Green and Colorado rivers. There is no hand of man controlling the water flow and during seasons of high snowmelt the Colorado produces the most violent whitewater in North America through the park. The Needles is pockmarked with massive buttes and isolated pinnacles. Desert troubadour Edward Abbey tried to put the majesty of the Canyonlands into words when he waxed rhapsodic that it is "the most weird, wonderful, magical place on earth—there is nothing else like it anywhere."

**WHERE/WHEN**

Utah/1964

**OFFICIAL POLICY REGARDING DOGS**

Activities for dogs are "very limited." No hiking trails, no backcountry and dogs can not even ride in four-wheel drive vehicles on undeveloped roads. Dogs can stay in campgrounds and walk on paved roads and that is it.

## What Your Dog Will Miss

At the Islands in the Sky District there are several easy trails along the top of the mesa to photograph destinations; in the Needles District there are a quartet of short, self-guided trails that can be accomplished with your dog in your vehicle on cool days. Aside from those there are hundreds of adventurous hiking miles that drop into the canyons to the Green and Colorado rivers that dogs will also never know.

# Nearby Places to Hike With Your Dog

Legend has it that cowboys once herded wild mustangs onto to the top of a mesa 2,000 feet above the Colorado River and blocked off their escape across a narrow neck of land with branches and brush, thus creating a natural corral. One time the horses in the corral were forgotten about and died of thirst while looking at the unaccessible river far below. So in 1959 when more than 5,000 acres, most of which are on the mesa top, were designated for a state park the incident was dredged up and Dead Horse Point State Park was born.

*About all your dog will see of the Canyonlands.*

While your dog will never trot the trails of Canyonlands National Park and look straight down 1000 feet at the confluence of the Green and Colorado rivers, she can get the same kind of experience next door in Dead Horse Point State Park. Two loops, connected by the Visitor Center, skirt the edges of the rim of the rock peninsula. Numerous short spur trails poke out to promontories overlooking the canyonlands (most are unfenced and provide no protection for overcurious canines). This is sparse desert land on top of the mesa and during a hot summer day

*Taking a break on Dead Horse Point.*

there is little shade and no natural drinking water on the trails for thirsty dogs. All told there are ten miles of paved and primitive trails at Dead Horse Point, most on hard, rocky paths.

A half-mile spur on the western side of the Dead Horse Point mesa leads to an overlook of Shafer Canyon. Across the canyon you can see an open plain that was used to film the famous final scene in the movie *Thelma & Louise* when Susan Sarandon drives a Thunderbird convertible over a cliff. Although there are wrecked automobiles in Shafer Canyon, they were placed there by the Bureau of Land Management to shore up the river bank. The wreckage from the movie was airlifted out of the canyon by helicopter.

# CAPITOL REEF
# NATIONAL PARK

## The Park

Capitol Reef is the youngest of Utah's five national parks, signed into existence by Richard Nixon on December 18, 1971. There were no paved roads into the area - known as Wayne Wonderland National Monument - until Route 24 was completed in 1962. The "reef" is a formation geologists call a monocline that is a steplike fold in the earth's rocky crust. The park's Waterpocket Fold rambles for over 100 miles, exposing alternating layers of brilliantly colored sandstone. The white Navajo Sandstone domes atop many of the cliffs along the Fremont River are rounded and look enough like the outline of the United States Capitol to give the park its name.

## What Your Dog Will Miss

In the middle of Utah's national park quintet Capitol Reef offers visitors willing to navigate unmaintained roads much of which is found in the Beehive State's other parks: slot canyons, colorful cliffs, sculpted rocks and natural bridge arches. There are a dozen or so day hikes along Utah Highway 24 and the

**WHERE/WHEN**

Utah/1971

**OFFICIAL POLICY REGARDING DOGS**

Dogs are not permitted on hiking trails. The only trail in the park where dogs can walk is the short, level path along the Fremont River between the campground and the visitor center. Your dog can also enjoy the historic orchards of Fruita and help pick fruit in season around the restored Gifford Farm House.

short Scenic Drive - the only paved routes through the park. Several, including trips to the deep canyon of Capitol Gorge, the serpentine Goosenecks cut into the gorge by the Fremont River and the slickrock of Sunset Point, can be completed with your dog in the car.

# Nearby Places to Hike With Your Dog

As Capitol Reef National Park rolls southward it pierces the two million acres of the Dixie National Forest, the largest national forest in Utah, and then the 1.9 million acres of the adjacent Grand Staircase-Escalante National Monument. There are hundreds and hundreds of

*Part of the rugged terrain of the Waterpocket Fold.*

miles of marked trails and wilderness here to hike with your dog.

Scenic Byway 12 runs south out of Capitol Reef through this mass of federally managed wilderness. First the winding two-lane road climbs Boulder Mountain to altitudes over 9,000 feet. The mountain itself reaches its peak at 11,313 feet on top of Blue Bell Knob, making this the highest forested plateau in North America. Innumerable forest roads and alpine trails are waiting for you and your dog through groves of quaking aspen, the Utah state tree.

As Scenic Byway 12 rolls into the Escalante Canyon it descends into hardrock canyon country. The Calf Creek Recreation Area, a Bureau of Land Management property, is the jumping off point for a 5.5-mile round-trip on a sandy trail to Lower Calf Creek Falls that spills 126 feet down a slickrock face into a cool, shady pool. The clear waters of Calf Creek have supported settlement for one thousand years and you can see pre-historic art sites and an ancient Anasazi peoples granary along the way.

Nearby the Escalante River Trailhead provides access to the "crookedest river in the world," as some of have tabbed it. In the dry months you can hike along with your dog can hike right through the

water under sandstone walls. Destinations include the Phipps Wash that leads to the 100-foot wide Phipps Arch and the smaller Maverick Natural Bridge. Backpackers can take your dog on an overnight trip 13 miles to the Escalante Natural Bridge and the Escalante Natural Arch a short distance further.

*Hiking along the Escalante River.*

# CARLSBAD CAVERNS
# NATIONAL PARK

## The Park

An ancient inland ocean from 250 million years ago evaporated and left behind some 300 limestone caves in a fossil reef of the Guadalupe Mountains, of which 119 are preserved in the national park. Three are show caves, the most famous being Carlsbad Caverns, the fifth largest subterranean chamber in North America with a ceiling 255 feet high. A cowboy named Jim White started exploring the caves with a handmade wire ladder in 1898 when he was a teenager. Despite his enthusiasm he could not convince the locals that there was anything to come see underground for over ten years. That was more than forty million visitors ago. The evening flight of Mexican free-tailed bats is the most famous in America although their numbers have declined drastically in recent years.

**WHERE/WHEN**
New Mexico/1930

**OFFICIAL POLICY REGARDING DOGS**
Dogs are not allowed on any trails or on any off roads or inside the cave.

## What Your Dog Will Miss

The underground displays are the star attraction at Carlsbad Caverns. The park does have three main hiking trails in the backcountry

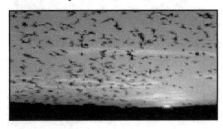

*The evening bat flight at Carlsbad Caverns.*

above ground that poke into the 33,000 acres of designated wilderness in the Chihuahuan Desert. Your dog will miss seeing the historic remains of guano mining around the caves in the unforgiving, shadeless desertscape of these hikes.

# Nearby Places to Hike With Your Dog

Your dog won't howl for the loss of Chihuahuan Desert hiking at Carlsbad Caverns with the 1.1 million acres of the Lincoln National Forest next door. The land is spread across three tracts and includes rambles among cool pines where elevations rise to 11,500 feet. Days of canine adventure await in any of the tracts; many trailheads are easily located just off main roads.

For a remote corner of the Southwest the Lincoln National Forest has provided American culture with two lasting icons. As law and order sorted itself out in 1878 and 1879, the Lincoln County Wars agitated America's largest county. A central figure in the conflict was a 17-year old hired gun named William Bonney. Imprisoned for extracting revenge on a sheriff's posse, Billy the Kid was detained in Lincoln before breaking out of jail and killing two guards. Bonney was soon hunted down and killed by Sheriff Pat Garrett.

*A dry wash makes a fine desert trail for dogs.*

The entire town of Lincoln - some 150 strong - is today a National Historic Landmark. You and your dog can walk through the one-street town, several blocks long, and study the historically preserved buildings that include the merchandise store owned by murdered Englishman John Tunstull and the courthouse where Billy the Kid made good his daring escape. After your walking tour you can pile the dog back in the car and take a driving tour on the 84-mile loop around Lincoln dubbed the Billy the Kid National Scenic Byway.

The Lincoln National Forest became famous around the world in May 1950 after an orphaned 5-pound bear cub was discovered clinging to a tree in a forest fire. The two-month old survivor was enlisted as the living symbol for Smokey the Bear, a cartoon caricature created six years earlier to preserve forests for use in World War II. While Smokey lived in the National Zoo in Washington D.C., he reportedly grew to be the second most beloved character in America, behind only Santa Claus. When Smokey died in 1976 he was returned to his home in Capitan, New Mexico and buried in a grave marked by a stone and plaque.

## The Park

Congaree National Park protects the largest contiguous area of old-growth bottomland hardwood forest remaining in the United States. More than 52 million acres of floodplain forests have been decimated in the southeastern United States in the past century making Congaree's 2,000 acres of virgin pine, tupelo and bald cypress special indeed. The park's forests harbor 20 state or national champion trees including loblolly pines, hickories and bald cypress. Newspaperman Harry Hampton began championing the protection of the water-logged forest in the 1950s. His campaign gained urgency when lumber prices rose in the 1960s making the hard-to-reach trees attractive to the Santee River Cypress Lumber Company that owned much of the land. An energetic grass roots effort brought federal protection in 1976.

**WHERE/WHEN**
South Carolina/2003

**OFFICIAL POLICY REGARDING DOGS**
Leashed dogs are permitted on all park trails. That is not a misprint.

## What Your Dog Will Miss

Nothing!

------------------------------------------------------------

# Nearby Places to Hike With Your Dog

The 150-foot high canopy of Congaree National Park is one of the highest deciduous roofs in the world. The marquee trail is a 2.4-mile *Boardwalk Loop* that lifts hikers above the flooding of the Congaree River that occurs an average of ten times a year. Underneath the boards are cypress knees protruding above the water line, mysterious swamp trademarks whose purpose is not entirely known.

Beyond the boardwalk the Congaree trail system pushes deeper into the old growth forest on wide, flat and almost always uncrowded trails. These loops provide trail time of several hours of easy going for your dog. You are never far from a waterway that lubricates the park and there is even a marked canoe trail that explores the meandering Cedar Creek. There are more than twenty miles of tail-friendly trails available to your dog in the park.

*Examinging blackwater swamp from the boardwalk.*

*The Congaree River floods several times each year, inundating the groves of cypress trees.*

# CRATER LAKE NATIONAL PARK

## The Park

One day about 7,500 years ago volcanic Mount Mazama erupted in an explosion scientists estimate was 42 times more powerful than Mount St. Helens in 1980. The mountain collapsed into itself forming a nearly symmetrical crater known as a caldera. Over the next seven millenia the crater filled with snowmelt from the 40 feet of snow the Cascades receive each year until the lake became the deepest in what is now the United States. Currently Crater Lake measures 1,943 feet deep. It is fed by no streams and water levels are affected only by evaporation and annual snowmelts. With an average depth of 1,148 feet it is the third deepest by average in the world. The brilliant blue color of the water and its dramatic setting cried out for making Crater Lake America's sixth national park. A century later Oregon, despite an embarrassment of natural wonders, has no other national park.

**WHERE/WHEN**
Oregon/1902

**OFFICIAL POLICY REGARDING DOGS**
Dogs are allowed only in developed areas; not on park trails or in the backcountry.

## What Your Dog Will Miss

Dogs can ride along in your vehicle around the 33-mile Rim Drive and get out at the observation points to stare down into the caldera but that is about it. Dogs can not use the *Cleetwood Cove Trail* that descends 700 feet to the water's edge nor can they hike the steep trail in the other direction to the top of Mount Scott, at 8,929 feet the highest point in the national park.

# Nearby Places to Hike With Your Dog

While Crater Lake receives all of the national publicity Oregonian outdoor enthusiasts flock to the shores of Diamond Lake, a short jaunt to the north, fives times as often. John Diamond, an early Oregon pioneer by way of Ireland and New York, first spotted the 3,015-acre lake in 1852 after summiting the nearby peak that also bears his name.

The result of glacial ice melt, the ancient lake is thought to have built up immunity to vaporization by volcanic eruptions thanks to an insulating layer of accumulated pumice on its floor from minor explosions.

*This is about as close as your dog can get to Crater Lake.*

In stark contrast to Crater Lake the waters of Diamond Lake average only 20 feet deep, shallow enough for a comfortable doggie swim in the summer. A paved path circumnavigates the lake for 11.5 miles but if you don't want to dodge the bicycles with your dog you can detour into the foot-traffic-only meadows surrounding Silent Creek, the lake's outlet to the north. The National Forest Service maintains four campgrounds around Diamond Lake.

Flanking Diamond Lake to the east and west are the volcanic shield mountains of Mount Bailey and Mount Thielsen. Dog-friendly trails lead up each prominent protrusion but the final climb to the distinctive pinnacle of 9,184-foot Mount Thielsen, known familiarly as the "Lightning Rod of the Cascades," requires technical climbing that will disqualify your dog from tagging the actual summit. On the positive side you meet up with the *Pacific Crest Trail* on the Mount Thielsen slopes.

*There's fun to be had even when you have to stick to the park roads.*

# CUYAHOGA VALLEY NATIONAL PARK

## The Park

Raise your hand if you knew that America's first national park of the 21st Century was created in.............Cleveland? To the first people who came here 12,000 years ago the Cuyahoga was the "crooked river." Its steep valley walls inhibited settlement as easterners poked into the region in the late 1700s. But a navigable water link between Lake Erie and the Ohio River was a priority in the early American Canal Age and in 1832 the Ohio & Erie Canal became a reality. The canal was put out of business by the Great Flood of 1913 and the Cuyahoga Valley was left to recreational purposes. The 33,000 acres along the banks of the Cuyahoga River were protected as a national recreation area so the heavy lifting for creating the park was done before its designation as a national park in 2000.

**WHERE/WHEN**
Ohio/2000

**OFFICIAL POLICY REGARDING DOGS**
Dogs are only banned from park buildings and boarding the Cuyahoga Valley Scenic Railroad.

## What Your Dog Will Miss

As befits its history as a recreation destination, Cuyahoga is a national park that permits dogs on its trails. It doesn't have the feel of the grand American national parks but instead evokes a comfortable familiarity on the trails that are squeezed between highways, farmlands and neighborhoods.

# Nearby Places to Hike With Your Dog

The main foot passage through the park is the nearly 20 miles of the *Towpath Trail* along the route of the historic canal. Ten trailheads make it easy to hike the crushed limestone path in biscuit-size chunks as it traverses meadows and forests and the remnants of locks and villages.

*Relaxing at the Happy Days Ledges.*

Another long-distance foot-path through the park is the *Buckeye Trail* that circles the entire state of Ohio for over 1200 miles. About 33 miles of the blue-blazed pathway wander the ravines and ridges of the valley.

Some of the best outings with your dog at the park are in the north end of the Cuyahoga Valley, in the Bradford Reservation. A five-mile all-purpose trail traverses the Tinkers Creek Gorge area, exploring Ohio's most spectacular canyon. The gorge is a National Natural Landmark, noted for its virgin hemlock forests. Short detours off the main trail include an easy walk to Bridal Veil Falls and the *Hemlock Creek Loop Trail*.

Other highlights include the dark and mysterious 2.2-mile ramble around the Ledges (from the Happy Day camp) and a short 1.25-mile loop through the Brandywine Gorge that takes your dog to the lip of Brandywine Falls and 160 feet down to the water level. For open-air hiking sign your dog up for a trip through the signature rolling Ohio countryside encountered on the *Horseshoe Pond/Tree Farm Trail*, a nearly three mile loop through meadows and around farmland.

*Brandywine Falls is a Cuyahoga Valley star.*

# DEATH VALLEY
# NATIONAL PARK

## The Park

Continental America's largest national park is an unforgiving collage of sand dunes, salt flats, bare mountains and badlands. The lowest point in North America is here at 282 feet below sea level in Badwater Basin. This is also the hottest and driest of all the national parks. Death Valley first received federal protection as a national monument in 1933, almost a century after it picked up its name from prospectors seeking a short cut to the northern California gold fields. Miners searched for precious ore here but never found anything other than borax which was hauled out of the valley in the 1880s for use in detergents and cosmetics by twenty-mule teams pulling the largest wagons ever designed to be transported by draft animals.

**WHERE/WHEN**
California/Nevada/1994

**OFFICIAL POLICY REGARDING DOGS**
Dogs can stay in all the park campgrounds but can not go on any hiking trails or into the wilderness.

## What Your Dog Will Miss

There really aren't that many hiking trails for your dog to miss out on; most of the hiking through Death Valley is trailless. Since dogs can hike on roads your trail buddy can get the Death Valley experience on backcountry dirt roads, many of which are barely two scars scratched into the desert. Some of the best lead into remote canyons like Echo Canyon Road, which features a two-

*Some hikes are not so bad to miss.*

mile canyon hike to a natural arch, and Twenty Mule Team Canyon Road that picks its way through scoured badlands for three miles. The twisting narrows of the Titus Canyon Road serve up stunning Death Valley scenery and views of the park's local herd of bighorn sheep. For canine hiking at higher elevations scout out the Chloride City Road.

------------------------------------------------------------

# Nearby Places to Hike With Your Dog

If you have ever watched a Hollywood western or the opening to the *Lone Ranger* you will recognize the Alabama Hills in Lone Pine, just west of Death Valley National Park, as you hike with your dog. The Alabama Hills consist of rounded, weathered granite boulders placed across a desert flatlands that form a sharp contrast with the sharply sculptured ridges of the nearby Sierra mountains. These majestic backdrops and rugged rock formations began attracting the attention of Hollywood, 212 miles to the west, in the 1920s.

You can hike with your dog along Movie Flat Road, a wide, dusty dirt cut through the Alabama Hills that is one of the most recognizable movie sets in Hollywood history. Beginning with Tom Mix in the silent era, every major Western star raced down the road on horseback at one time or another. Roy Rogers appeared here in his first starring role in *Under Western Stars* and Bill Boyd, known on the screen as Hopalong Cassidy, filmed so many roles in Lone Pine that he moved here.

Although the golden age for Lone Pine has gone the way of the Hollywood western, film crews occasionally still appear. *Bad Day at Black Rock* (Spencer Tracy/Robert Ryan) used the area to build an entire town along the railroad tracks in 1955 and, more recently, Fred Ward and Kevin Bacon battled giant earthworms in the Alabama Hills in *Tremors*. So keep an eye out for movie crews. Your dog may be the next big star.

*Hiking in the hoofprints of the Lone Ranger and Silver.*

# DENALI NATIONAL PARK

## The Park

"Denali" is a native Athabaskan word meaning "the high one" or "the great one." Either way Mount McKinley, the star of the park, certainly fits the bill. At 20,237 feet the massif is more than 4,000 feet higher than any of its neighboring peaks. From some angles you can see 18,000 feet from the base to the peak - the largest of any mountain on earth. The main summit was first scaled in 1913 and tagging its top remains one of mountaineering's great prizes. More than 1,000 people try each year, about 600 make it and over the years more than 100 have never come home. A gold prospector named William Dickey called it Mount McKinley when William McKinley, the last veteran of the Civil War to serve in the Executive Office, was running

**WHERE/WHEN**
Alaska/1917

**OFFICIAL POLICY REGARDING DOGS**
Dogs are not permitted on the park trails (with two exceptions) or in the wilderness, which comprises over 95 percent of the park.

for President in 1896. The national park, with more than six million acres, assumed the native name and over the years the mountain is called that as often as not.

## What Your Dog Will Miss

The chance to see America's only 20,000-foot mountain, mostly. The park has only a single 92-mile road and only the first 15 miles of that are open to unpermitted private vehicles. The only place along that stretch to glimpse the continent's tallest peak is on the *Mountain Vista Trail* where dogs are barred. Only the top few thousand feet are visible at this point, 72 miles away so human visitors are only seeing a fraction more on this trail than your dog back in the car.

After the Savage River at the 15-mile mark the Park Road trundles on unpaved (due to permafrost concerns) and plied mainly by shuttle buses. This is a chance to get out and hike with your dog in the great Alaskan outdoors up the road. You won't be able to hike far enough to ever see the iconic mountain (the first base to summit view does not come until the 62-mile mark) but the scenery and lack of activity (save for the shuttle buses) are rewards in themselves.

*The view hiking up the 92-mile Park Road.*

The two paths where your dog is allowed to walk are the *Bike Path* and the *Roadside Trail* which parallels the Park Road for almost two miles from the visitor center to the park headquarters. This pleasant ramble explores a boreal forest of white and black spruce with groves of quaking aspen sprinkled in for color. It won't make a national park highlight film but is more leg stretching than your dog is used to in America's national parks.

---

# Nearby Places to Hike With Your Dog

On the eastern boundary of Denali National Park is Denali State Park. At 325,000 acres the Alaska state property is dwarfed by its larger neighbor but still almost half the size of Rhode Island. The views of Mount McKinley from the state park are sublime - Alaskan officials have even provided telescopes that are pointed directly at the hulking mountain. You can hike anywhere with your dog in Denali State Park and once you get into the backcountry your dog can run off leash while under voice control.

On the northern edge of Denali sits Bus 142, the abandoned Fairbanks City Transit System bus that Christopher McCandless starved to death inside while attempting to survive in the Alaskan wilderness in 1992. The incident was popularized in a book by Jon Krakauer and a movie by Sean Penn, *Into the Wild*. Bus 142 sits beside the *Stampede Trail* that was begun as a mining trail in the 1930s. The trail was upgraded in the 1960s but the road was never finished (the abandoned bus had been used to transport workers). The *Stampede Trail* is accessed at milepost 251.1 of the George Parks Highway (Alaska Route 3), two miles north of the borough of Healy. After driving as far as possible on the *Stampede Trail* the pilgrimage to the backcountry "Magic Bus" site can be made by backpacking in with your dog.

# EVERGLADES
# NATIONAL PARK

## The Park

The Everglades is America's tropical wilderness. The original wetlands were once five times as large as the area the park now protects, disgorging water from Lake Okeechobee in a slow-moving discharge that gave rise to its description as a "River of Grass." Still the largest wilderness east of the Mississippi River with 1.5 million acres, the unique Everglades ecosystem is so irreplaceable it has been declared an International Biosphere Reserve. That mangrove ecosystem is the largest in the western hemisphere and countless animals and birds exist only in the forests and swamps of southern Florida, including the American crocodile and the elusive state animal, the Florida panther.

## What Your Dog Will Miss

Everglades trails explore slight rises in the "river of grass" that have developed into tree islands known as hammocks. The two most prominent areas for hiking are the pinelands of Long Pine Key which harbors some 200 species of sub-tropical plants and the coastal prairie around the Flamingo Visitor Center at the end of the park road. Your dog will also not be able to enjoy the park canoe trails.

**WHERE/WHEN**

Florida/1934

**OFFICIAL POLICY REGARDING DOGS**

Dogs can be in the campgrounds and picnic areas, on roadways that carry "public vehicular traffic" and on maintained grounds around public facilities. And dogs can ride on your boat. That's it.

*Tail-wagging times at an Everglades picnic area.*

# Nearby Places to Hike With Your Dog

A sliver of the south Florida swamp forest twenty miles long by five miles wide has been cut out and served as the Fakahatchee Strand Preserve State Park. Dogs are welcome on the trails of "the Amazon of North America," as they are in all Florida state parks. That includes the half-mile *Big Cypress Bend Boardwalk* that stabs into the interior of the world's only Bald Cypress-Royal Palm forest.

Another chunk of the Florida wetlands open to your dog south of Interstate 75 is the Picayune Strand State Forest. Most of the forest is the remnant of the Golden Gate Estates, a 57,000-acre post-World War II residential development that was planned to be the largest in America. Prospective buyers were flown over the site during the dry season to scout lots, unaware that nothing could ever be developed since the land would be underwater in the summer flood season. Thus was born the notorious "selling swampland in Florida" scam.

*Florida state parks and forests
welcome dogs to trails.*

## The Park

The Great Northern Railway was the driving force in the creation of Glacier National Park, building hotels and chalets in the majestic Rocky Mountains they called the "Crown of the Continent." For many years the railroad provided the only access to the national park. Today many of those historic lodges have been preserved as landmarks. Unfortunately, the namesake glaciers can not be similarly managed. Back in the middle of the 1800s there were believed to be 150 glaciers in the parks; today there are only 25 active glaciers and their continued existence is in extreme jeopardy.

## What Your Dog Will Miss

Over 700 miles of trails. There will be no day hikes for your dog along the signature Going-to-the-Sun Road that is the only road that traverses the park. When construction began in 1921 this was the first project undertaken by the National Park Service to cater to the new breed of automobile tourist. It took twelve years to carve the two-lane road 53 miles across the Continental Divide at Logan Pass. There won't be any rides for your dog on the vintage 1930s-era park tour buses known as Red Jammers either.

**WHERE/WHEN**

Montana/1910

**OFFICIAL POLICY REGARDING DOGS**

Dogs are not allowed on any park trails (save for the short paved bike path between Apgar and West Glacier when it is is snow-free) and they can not enjoy the shores around the park's 130 named lakes. Dogs can ride in your boat however. They can also stay in frontcountry campgrounds and attend your picnics.

# Nearby Places to Hike With Your Dog

Abutting Glacier National Park on the Canadian side of the border is Waterton Lakes National Park. The two parks have been co-joined into the Waterton-Glacier International Peace Park that is the first ever such effort. The two parks share much of the same stunning Rocky Mountain scenery and wildlife. In fact the only thing you will see in Waterton National Park that you won't see in Glacier National Park is dogs on the trail.

Canada has the same crush of summer tourists in its national parks as the United States. Canada has the same concerns for the safety and welfare of wildlife in its national parks as the United States. And yet dogs are welcome on the trails in all of Canada's national parks - it is considered such a natural activity that the parks mostly don't even address the issue.

Waterton actually pre-dates Glacier as a national park. It was created in 1895 - the fourth park set aside by the Canadian Federation in its first three decades of existence. Upper Waterton Lake is the deepest lake in the Canadian Rockies and the star of the park where the Prince of Wales railway hotel was built as a resort in 1927. Waterton is the smallest of the Canaidan Rockies national parks and the country's only park that preserves fescue grasslands like those that blanket the foothills.

A view from the road is the best your dog will be able to do in Glacier National Park.

Waterton Lakes National Park is laced with easy-to-complete day hikes below and above the treeline that access waterfalls in the Red Rock Canyon and secluded lakes beyond the Akamina Parkway. Mount Blackiston is the park's roof at 9,550 feet. The 2.5-mile *Lineham Creek Trail* runs along its southern slopes and experienced scramblers can ascend the rubble rock to the top. Some Waterton trails like the *Lakeshore Trail* connect to Glacier National Park - remember not to allow your dog to cross into that forbidden land.

# GRAND CANYON NATIONAL PARK

## The Park

The sheer audaciousness of the Grand Canyon has left many a visitor fumbling for words to describe it. When Theodore Roosevelt visited as President in 1903 he took his best oratorical shot by saying, "The Grand Canyon fills me with awe. It is beyond comparison - beyond description." He concluded by stating that the handiwork of the Colorado River is "the one great sight which every American should see." Legislation to make the Grand Canyon a national park had existed since 1882 but it was not until 1919, mere weeks after Roosevelt's death at the age of 60, that Woodrow Wilson signed the paperwork to make the Grand Canyon America's 15th national park.

## What Your Dog Will Miss

Unless your dog is sporting a convincing mule costume, any hiking in the canyon will be missed. One place your dog may not have to miss is Shoshone Point, a permit-only section of the canyon that is reserved for weddings and the like. Check with the park office and if there are no special events scheduled you can hike with your dog along the one-mile dirt road through Ponderosa pines and

**WHERE/WHEN**

Arizona/1919

**OFFICIAL POLICY REGARDING DOGS**

Dogs are not allowed on trails below the rim at the Grand Canyon but there is a surprising amount of canine hiking you can do otherwise considering the immense popularity of the park. Dogs are allowed on all the trails (12 miles of them) throughout the developed areas of the South Rim. The less visited North Rim is also less inviting for canine hikers. You can get the dog only on a bridle path between the lodge and the *North Kaibab Trail.*

through high country meadows to one of the most photographed edges of the Grand Canyon.

---------------------------------------------------------------

# Nearby Places to Hike With Your Dog

Downstream from the Grand Canyon the hand of man went to work to create its own magic on the Colorado River in the 1930s. Still one of the man-made wonders of the world, the Hoover Dam remains high on the list of America's greatest engineering triumphs. Many of the techniques employed in its construction had never been tried before and 112 men lost their lives in order to plug the Colorado River in the Black Canyon. The 726-foot high Hoover Dam is still the second highest dam in America (only the Oroville Dam in California is higher and it is earth fill) and the river backs up 110 miles behind it to fill Lake Mead, the country's largest man-made reservoir.

Millions of people come to vacation in the Lake Mead National Recreation Area above and below the dam, a water playground smack in the middle of an unforgiving desert. Your dog is welcome to join the fun-seekers on the water and in the campgrounds. The vast majority of acreage in the park is not under water, however. A rewarding trip plan at Lake Mead to experience the eastern fringes of the Mojave Desert is to drive to the various tail-friendly short hikes that have been created by the park service around the lake.

Experienced canine hikers will want to explore the canyons and washes of the designated wilderness areas of the desert. This is rough, steep terrain and during the summer temperatures can reach 120 degrees so the best time to log this on your dog's trip planner is between November and March.

*Mules are OK inside the Grand Canyon, dogs not OK.*

## The Park

The rocks that make up the Teton Range are the oldest in the National Park Service system - estimated to be about 2.7 billion years. The tallest mountain, Grand Teton, lends the park its name and is the second highest point in Wyoming. The jagged Teton peaks rise spectacularly above the flat Jackson Hole river valley and frame a series of glacial lakes that stretch through the park. The national park, just ten miles south of Yellowstone National Park, was set up to protect the major peaks as John Rockefeller, Jr. began purchasing the surrounding land to contribute to the park. Today the two John D. Rockefeller, Jr. Memorial Parkway follows the Snake River between the two parks.

## What Your Dog Will Miss

By walking the roads of the developed area of the park your dog will have fantastic views of the Grand Teton Range across the lakes but will never be able to hike into them. Park officials even provide Mutt Mitt stations on the grounds.

------------------------------------

**WHERE/WHEN**
Wyoming/1929

**OFFICIAL POLICY REGARDING DOGS**
Dogs are prohibited on the trail and in the Teton backcountry. Dogs also can not go on the swimming beaches or ride in any boats on park waters, save for Jackson Lake. Dogs can go anywhere a car can go but not more than 30 feet from pavement. Come November dogs can trot along some of the park roads that close for the winter-use season. Dogs are never allowed on the park's multi-use pathway.

# Nearby Places to Hike With Your Dog

On the doorstep of the Tetons is the Bridger-Teton National Forest, comprising 3.4 million acres that make it the third largest federally managed forest outside of Alaska. Wyoming's tallest mountain, Gannett Peak, is here but offers one of the hardest mountaineering challenges in the United States. But there are over 40 other named mountains over 12,000 feet in the forest for canine hikers seeking alpine routes. Huckleberry Mountain, a ten-mile round trip from 7,000 feet to 9,615 feet, serves up views of both Grand Teton and Yellowstone national parks from an abandoned fire lookout built by the Works Progress Administration in 1938; the trailhead is off the Rockefeller Parkway at Flag Ranch.

The Gros Ventre Road east of the park leads to a spot on Sheep Mountain unique in geologic history. In 1925 a hunk of the mountain containing 50 million cubic yards of debris slid down into the valley with such force it rode 300 feet up the opposite slope. The Gros Ventre Slide is one of the most visible geologic scars on earth. An interpretive trail explores the 90-year old debris pile that plugged the Gros Ventre River and created five-mile long Lower Slide Lake.

*With more than three million dog-friendly acres roads like this one in Bridger-Teton National Forest are easy to find.*

# GREAT BASIN NATIONAL PARK

## The Park

In 1986 *Life* magazine anointed Route 50 that runs east-west through Nevada as "The Loneliest Road in America." Just about the loneliest stretch of that lonely road runs by Great Basin National Park. Almost all of Nevada lies in the Great Basin, an arid topographic region between the Sierra Nevada mountains to the west and the Wasatch range to the east. This representative sample of the Great Basin began its long journey to national park status in the 1920s when protection was afforded to highly decorative marble caverns discovered by Absalom Lehman back in 1885. When Lehman Caves National Monument opened in 1922 it greeted 63 visitors in its first year.

## What Your Dog Will Miss

Most people make the journey to remote Great Basin and take the 12-mile Wheeler Peak Scenic Drive which your dog can do - and maybe even enjoy the smells of the pinyon-juniper forest through an open car window - and experience Lehman Caves which your dog can not do. Your dog can also leave unchecked the park's ancient Bristlecone Pines and Nevada's only glacier from her sightseeing list from the trail.

**WHERE/WHEN**
Nevada/1986

**OFFICIAL POLICY REGARDING DOGS**
No dogs permitted on trails or in the backcountry. They can walk a bit on the roads in the campgrounds and the parking lots at the visitor centers. The only exceptions are the *Baker Trail* at the Great Basin Visitor Center and the *Lexington Arch Trail*, neither of which is actually inside the park. Well, the unique limestone Lexington Arch (most desert arches are sandstone) is in the very southeast corner of Great Basin but most of the rocky 1.7-mile trail is not.

# Nearby Places to Hike With Your Dog

In 2006 a 68,000-acre swath of Nevada Great Basin right next to the national park and about the same size was designated as the Highland Ridge Wilderness under the auspices of the Bureau of Land Management. You would be hard pressed to tell whether the pinyon-juniper covered mountains and rocky ridges and Bristlecone Pine stumps are part of the national park or the wilderness area. Elevations rise from 6,070 feet to 10,825 feet. There are not many formal marked trails (the *Lexington Arch Trail* is one) but the primitive and unconfined solitude of Highland Ridge is all dog-friendly. There are 59 miles of off-road vehicle routes; backpackers can tackle the 16.8-mile namesake *Highland Ridge Trail*.

*The Great Basin is where dogs come to cut their own trails.*

*There is plenty of room for dogs to romp in the Great Basin desert.*

# GREAT SAND DUNES NATIONAL PARK

## The Park

About 900 miles from the nearest ocean are the highest sand dunes in North America. Souvenirs from melting glaciers and Rio Grande River deposits 60 square miles of sand has been blown up against the western flanks of the Sangre de Cristo Mountains. Explorer Zebulon Pike made the first American observations of the dunes in 1807. When prospectors were turning over every rock in the West in the late 1800s there was speculation that gold was washed into the dunes along with sand. Minute particles were discovered - enough that mining operations were set up during the tough times of the Great Depression, spurring calls for government protection. It took over 70 years for the status of the Great Dunes to shift from monument to national park. Sound measures taken by the National Park Service have proven Great Dunes to be the quietest national park in the Lower 48 - although not on May and June weekends when it is just like a beach day in the park.

**WHERE/WHEN**

Colorado/2004

**OFFICIAL POLICY REGARDING DOGS**

Dogs can enjoy any parts of the day-use area in Great Sand Dunes National Park. That means the first mile-and-a-half of the dunefield (essentially up to the first 700-foot ridge) and the *Montville Nature Trail* that loops into the lower slopes of the Sangre de Cristo Mountains. Dogs are not allowed in the backcountry, either in the dunefield or the mountains.

## What Your Dog Will Miss

Dogs can not make any of the alpine hikes at Great Dunes, most notably tagging the summit of 13,297-foot Mount Herard. Your dog will also not be able to spend the

night in the dunes since camping is only allowed in the backcountry of the dunefield. That also counts out a trip to Star Dune, at 750 feet, the highest sand dune on the continent.

---------------------------------------------------------------

# Nearby Places to Hike With Your Dog

Right here. You can spend hours hiking with your dog in the Great Dunes, up and down the slopes, across the ridges. High Dune, about 699 feet high, is an hour's hike from the parking lot. The temperatures in the sand can reach 150 degrees in the summer months so plan your dog's day accordingly. Medano Creek is a seasonal creek that flows through the sand in front of the dunefield for your dog to splash in; the water can be a foot or higher in May and June at its most energetic flow.

Both Great Dunes National Park and neighboring San Luis State Park have unconfined hiking for your dog through grasslands on the fringes of the dunes. The state park has a campground under the dunefield; the Zapata Falls Recreation Area south of the dunes also has camping. The main attraction there are the falls that make a powerful 25-foot plunge inside a rock crevice. Although the hike is short - barely half a mile - your dog's four-wheel drive will come in handy when scrambling across slippery rocks and through chilly water. In the winter Zapata Falls freezes into a sensuous column of ice and the hike is on a frozen river until well into springtime.

*The Great Sand Dunes are great times for dogs.*

# GREAT SMOKY MOUNTAINS NATIONAL PARK

## The Park

With the coming of the railroads in the mid-1800s the southern Appalachian highlands were logged so aggressively that it set off alarm bells. After the National Park Service formed in 1916 one of its goals was a park in the Eastern United States near where most of the country lived. But the government did not own land like it did out West for parks and money was scarce to go on a land buying spree. But well-heeled large donors like John Rockefeller, Jr. and private citizens in North Carolina and Tennessee began the slow process of acquiring land in the 1920s. By 1934 the government had acquired enough land on the mountains and in the hollows to begin cutting trails and building fire towers. Today Great Smoky Mountains National Park (the name comes from a perpetual haze courtesy of water and hydrocarbons produced by the air-breathing leaves of the deciduous forest) covers 800 square miles and is America's busiest park. With nine million visitors each year Great Smoky draws more than twice as many people as any other national park.

**WHERE/WHEN**
North Carolina-
Tennessee/1934

**OFFICIAL POLICY REGARDING DOGS**
Dogs are allowed in campgrounds, picnic areas and along roads. They can also go on two paths where bikes are shuffled off to as well - the 1.5-mile *Oconaluftee River Trail* near the visitor center in Cherokee, North Carolina and the 1.9-mile *Gatlinburg Trail* in Tennessee near the Sugarlands Visitor Center. That's it for dogs in America's most popular national park.

## What Your Dog Will Miss

More than 850 miles of trails. That includes the *Appalachian Trail* that runs over 6,643-foot Clingmans Dome that is the highest point on the entire 2,130-mile footpath. Only three places on the entire trail deny access to dogs - Baxter State Park at the northern terminus in Maine, Bear Mountain State Park Trailside Museum in New York which provides an alternate path, and Great Smoky Mountains National Park.

A unique feature of the national park are the high elevation heath balds that are treeless expanses found primarily in the Southern Appalachians, where the climate is too warm to support an alpine zone - upper areas where trees fail to grow due to short or non-existent growing seasons - even at the highest elevations. Why some summits are bald and some are not is a mystery to scientists. There are two types of balds - heath balds with blankets of evergreen shrubs and grassy balds covered with dense swards of native grasses.

------------------------------------------------------------

# Nearby Places to Hike With Your Dog

Fortunately for dogs in the Southern Highlands balds are not exclusive to Great Smoky Mountains National Park. If you follow the Blue Ridge Parkway north to Milepost 420 (the southern terminus of the Parkway is at the entrance to the park) you reach Black Balsam Knob in the Pisgah National Forest. A short ten-minute climb pulls you above the balsam firs for hiking across the 6,214-foot grassy bald and neighboring Tennant Mountain with unobstructed views of the Blue Ridge Mountains for your dog almost every step of the way. Matching canine hiking on Black Balsam Knob stride for stride in "wow" moments is the moderate climb to the Sam Knob summit on the opposite side of the trailhead lot.

*Black Balsam Knob.*

When the *Appalachian Trail* leaves Great Smoky Mountains National Park it soon reaches Max Patch Mountain, one of the favorite hikes near Asheville, a mountain town known for its love of good hiking. Max Patch was a farmer in the 1800s who cleared the 4,629-foot high mountaintop for his cattle to graze; it is today the southernmost bald on the *Appalachian Trail* and often referred to as one of its "crown jewels." But it is not a natural bald - the Forest Service keeps the peak grassy with tractors.

# GUADALUPE MOUNTAINS NATIONAL PARK

## The Park

Before Wallace Pratt was hired as the first petroleum geologist at Humble Oil & Refining Company in 1918 the oil industry operated mostly on "dig-and-hope" technology. In a long career Pratt, who would be named Grand Old Man of Exploration in 1976, proved the value of geology in finding oil many times over. He spent his spare time east of El Paso, Texas in the Guadalupe Mountains, an oddity among mountain ranges since they had once been the underground reef of an inland sea. Pratt donated the first 5,000 acres for the national park that adjoins more celebrated Carlsbad Caverns in the same mountain range.

## What Your Dog Will Miss

Your dog will never have a chance to sit on the roof of Texas or put a pawprint in the register at the end of the 4.2-mile trail up 8,751-foot Guadalupe Peak. There are another 80 miles or so of trails in the lightly-visited park, including the ones in McKittrick Canyon with the only surface water of note in the mountains, that your best trail buddy will never sniff.

**WHERE/WHEN**
Texas/1972

**OFFICIAL POLICY REGARDING DOGS**
Aside from a pair of service trails at the visitor center dogs are not allowed on any trails or in the backcountry. They can go into campgrounds and picnic areas. That includes any of the trails in Dog Canyon.

# Nearby Places to Hike With Your Dog

Public land is scarce in West Texas but you can scoot over the state line into New Mexico for a doggy adventure in White Sands National Monument. Dogs have long been welcome on the mystical white sands of southern New Mexico. When America's space age began at White Sands Missile Range with the firing of a Tiny Tim test booster on September 26, 1945, it was important to retrieve small missile parts to analyze success or failure. These searches routinely wasted countless man-hours as ground recovery crews scoured vast expanses of desert for often-buried missile fragments.

That ended in 1961 with the introduction of the Missile Dogs: Dingo, a Weimaraner, and Count, a German Shorthair. For up to a year before firing, important components of a missile were sprayed with squalene, a shark-liver oil that the dogs could smell from hundreds of feet away. After a missile firing, Dingo and Count raced among

*The White Sands are a giant sandbox for dogs.*

the sands sniffing out the scent objects. With a 96% recovery rate, the program was so successful that other military and scientific agencies requested the services of the original Missile Dogs of White Sands.

Today you can hike with your dog anywhere in the giant sandbox that is White Sands National Monument. The world's largest gypsum sand dunes form when the mineral dissolves in nearby mountains during rainstorms. Instead of being carried off by a river (this is an arid environment) wind transports the crystals where they accumulate in brilliantly white sand dunes.

White Sands offers 6.2 miles of marked dog-friendly trails but there is no need to limit your explorations. Any dune is open to a canine hike. Stay alert for reptiles and rodents scampering on the dunes that have adapted to the white sands and are now a funny bleached white color. During the heat of summer, try a night hike - when the moon is full, the park, located in New Mexico on U.S. Highway 70 between Alamogordo and Las Cruces, stays open until midnight. The desert cools off then and the sands are haunting by moonlight.

# HOT SPRINGS
# NATIONAL PARK

## The Park

The water that bubbles to the ground at 143 degrees Farenheit fell to earth 4,000 years ago, percolating deep into the earth and heating four degrees every 300 feet before seeping out of the lower west slope of Hot Springs Mountain. Spanish explorers and French trappers visited the springs for centuries. In 1832 the federal government made its first stab at the national park concept by reserving land around the springs but nothing was done to back up the designation and private bathhouses flourished in the tourist mecca. In 1921 Hot Springs was elevated to national park status and carries on now as a unique protective cocktail of historic small city and park.

**WHERE/WHEN**
Arkansas/1921

**OFFICIAL POLICY REGARDING DOGS**
Hot Springs National Park is proudly dog-friendly.

## What Your Dog Will Miss

About the only thing your dog will miss at Hot Springs is a long soak in a bathhouse.

-------------------------------------------------------------

# Nearby Places to Hike With Your Dog

There are more than 30 miles of top-notch hiking trails available in Hot Springs, mostly on short, inter-connecting jogs on the low-lying, rounded Hot Springs Mountain and West Mountain that flank the city. Many of these paths were carved for visitors who were encouraged to walk daily in addition to their baths as part of an all-encompassing healthy routine at the spas. Most were constructed wide enough to

*Stopping by one of the 47 hot springs in the national park.*

handle carriages and are still roomy today. Although the mountains only top out at little more than 1,000 feet expect to find some climbs that will leave you and your dog panting. Also, there aren't many streams so make sure you carry plenty of cooling water for your dog on a summer afternoon's outing.

For extended canine hiking head out on the *Sunset Trail* that leaves West Mountain and tags Music Mountain at 1,405 feet (the highest spot in the park) before doubling back onto Sugarloaf Mountain. This trail doesn't loop and is a good candidate for a car shuttle. Back in town you can take your dog on a tour of Bathhouse Row with a half-mile saunter down the Promenade, visiting several of the 47 springs that flow at an average rate of 850,000 gallons a day.

Just as Hot Springs is the first national park in the South its neighbor, the Ouachita National Forest, is the oldest national forest in the southern United States. Begun as the Arkansas National Forest the Ouachita now comprises 65,000 acres and six wilderness areas. The star of the forest is the 223-mile long *Ouachita National Recreation Trail* that is a backpacking route that runs all the way into Oklahoma through the mountains that never rise higher than 2,753 feet.

*Out for a stroll on the Promenade as guests to Hot Springs have done for well over a century.*

# JOSHUA TREE NATIONAL PARK

## The Park

The land of the grotesquely-shaped members of the arboreal Yucca family has been protected since the 1930s but did not achieve national park status until 1994. Most of the park - larger in size than Rhode Island - is wilderness and boasts some of the most enchanting rock formations in southern California. Joshua Tree National Park consists of the high desert of the Mojave and the lower elevations of the Colorado Desert that spreads across the eastern half of the park. Creosote bushes and ocotillo and cholla cactus are the botanical stars here. The namesake Joshua tree is much in evidence in the open areas of the Mojave desert section of the park. It was so-named by Mormon settlers in the 1800s who thought the fibrous branches looked as if they were lifted to the sky in prayer.

**WHERE/WHEN**
California/1994

**OFFICIAL POLICY REGARDING DOGS**
Dogs are never allowed on trail and can never be more than 100 feet from a road, picnic area or campground.

## What Your Dog Will Miss

The paved park road leads to most of the major Joshua Tree attractions and short nature walks your dog will see only from the car window. Chief among them are Barker Dam that was used by early cattle ranchers; Hidden Valley that legend says was used by rustlers eyeing those cattle; Indian Cove that features one of the park's several water-tinged oases and the vegetatively dense Cholla Cactus Garden.

--------------------------------------------------------------

# Nearby Places to Hike With Your Dog

In many ways San Bernadino National Forest sounds like a national park. Its value as a natural treasure was recognized back in the 19th century when President Benjamin Harrison set aside 737,280 acres of the San Bernadino Mountains that had been gouged and grazed since gold was discovered there in 1855. The forest has signature attractions like Big Bear Lake, 36-mile long Deep Creek and bighorn sheep. It also boasts two scenic drives: the 67-mile

*Joshua trees are fun to look at but don't offer much shade to a hot trail dog.*

Palms to Pine Scenic Byway that takes in the rugged desert and the snow-dressed, 11,000-foot mountain peaks and the 110-mile Rim of the World Scenic Byway. And San Bernadino draws more visitors than either Yellowstone or Yosemite.

But fortunately for dog owners the San Bernadino National Forest, across Interstate 10 from Joshua Tree National Park, developed under the guidance of the U.S. Forestry Service. So that means 500 miles of paw-friendly trails, minus some that lie in the San Jacinto State Wilderness and Santa Rosa and San Jacinto Mountains National Monument. One of the highlights is the Heaps Peak Arboretum that sits at 6,000 feet in the mountains, one of the highest elevated "tree museums" in the country. The marquee hike in the arboretum is along the easy-going *Sequoia Trail* that travels through groves of Arizona cypress, quaking aspen and giant sequoias.

# KENAI FJORDS
# NATIONAL PARK

## The Park

The park was created to provide safe harbor for the Harding Icefield whose more than 700 square miles of ice disgorge almost 40 glaciers. The fjords are glacial valleys gouged by the icefield that have dented the east coast of the Kenai Peninsula. Most of the park is visited only by cruises or flight-seeing trips hat depart from the town of Seward but there is road access to a single glacier - Exit Glacier.

## What Your Dog Will Miss

Short, wooded trails lead to overlooks of the retreating Exit Glacier and a 4.1-mile *Harding Icefield Trail* leads beyond the forests and meadows to high above the treeline before the trail ends on bare rock before an endless (for now) panorama of ice and snow.

**WHERE/WHEN**
Alaska/1980

**OFFICIAL POLICY REGARDING DOGS**
Unless your dog is mushing or skijoring he can not leave the parking lot of the Exit Glacier Nature Center.

*You can take exactly one more hike in Kenai Fjords than your dog - the trail to the edge of Exit Glacier.*

# Nearby Places to Hike With Your Dog

Kenai Fjords National Park is surrounded by more than five million acres of the Chugach National Forest. The Chugach is known for its bald eagle population which is considered greater than the number of all the bald eagles living in the Lower 48. The closest dog-friendly trail to the national park is near the entrance off Exit Glacier Road where the *Resurrection River Trail* is a narrow ribbon through dense spruce forests for 16 miles, although travel becomes primitive past the four-mile mark.

The Seward Highway runs down the Kenai Peninsula 130 miles from Anchorage and enters the national forest at the town of Portage. From there the road, a National Scenic Highway, slides 72 miles through the Chugach National Forest; there are trailheads for day hikes all the way to the national park in Seward and also down the Sterling Highway on its journey to Homer on the western coast of the Kenai Peninsula.

*Any type of hike is on your dog's menu in the Chugach National Forest from romps in the meadows beneath the mountains to climbs up the peaks.*

# LASSEN VOLCANIC NATIONAL PARK

## The Park

Lassen Volcanic Park is one of the few spots on earth where all four types of volcano - plug dome, shield, cinder cone and strato - can be found; the namesake Lassen Peak is the largest plug dome volcano on earth. The geothermal wonders were recognized early on and Theodore Roosevelt created a national monument here in 1907. After a series of eruptions on Lassen Peak began in 1914 Lassen was upgraded to a national park.

## What Your Dog Will Miss

The spitting mudpots and stinking fumaroles and boiling springs of geothermal regions like the Sulphur Works, Devil's Kitchen and Bumpass Hell will all be scratched off your dog's itinerary. So will the park's 150 miles of trails. The 30-mile Lassen Volcanic National Park Highway is the highest road in the Cascade Mountains as it climbs to 8,512 feet, allowing your dog excellent views of all that will be missed close up.

**WHERE/WHEN**
California/1916

**OFFICIAL POLICY REGARDING DOGS**
Dogs are not allowed on any hiking trail or in the backcountry or in any body of the water or inside any building. Don't let your dog's paw off the pavement.

-------------------------------------------------------------

# Nearby Places to Hike With Your Dog

Due west of Lassen Volcanic National Park, on the opposite side of the town of Redding, is old gold mining country that lives on as Whiskeytown National Recreation Area. Dogs are allowed to trot all 24 trails in the park but must avoid swimming beaches along the centerpiece lake. The park's waterfalls make worthy destinations: the *Carr Trail*, two years in the making, opened the way to the 220-foot Whiskeytown Falls that was not discovered until 2004; Boulder Creek Falls that tumbles 138 feet in three drops into a box canyon can be reached by traveling one mile from Mill Creek Road; and Brandy Creek Falls requires a sporty three-mile round trip to soak in its series of wide cascades.

While you are in the mood for hunting waterfalls track down the hydro-spectaculars in the nearby Shasta National Forest on the McCloud River. The trail at McCloud Falls reveals three waterfalls in little more than a mile: the Lower Falls (a powerful, ten-foot drop into a wide pool), the Middle Falls (a classically wide, 50-foot waterfall), and the Upper Falls (a water spout squeezing through granite cliffs). At McCloud Falls be on the lookout for the little American Dipper birds that patrol the tumbling waters. These tiny birds, also known as water ouzels, zoom around over the surface and plunge in and out of the cascading water in search of food. They use their wings to "fly" underwater and can even be seen walking on the stream bottom pecking for larval insects, fish eggs and even slow fish just as if they were walking on the trail.

*Looking down at the Middle Falls of the St. Cloud River.*

Even for a state celebrated for its natural wonders, Mount Shasta stands out. Literally. The 14,179-foot volcanic peak features almost 10,000 feet of prominence. It can be seen from 140 miles away around Northern California. Put another way, if Mount Shasta were in Philadelphia you could see its snow-capped ridges from the Empire State Building in New York City and the Washington Monument in Washington, D.C. Ash Creek Falls tumbles 330 feet down a rock face on Mount Shasta's eastern slopes of the volcano, framed by the summit in the background.

The railroad town of Dunsmuir eight miles south of Mount Shasta does not disappoint on the waterfall checklist either. In the northern part of town Hedge Creek makes its final plunge to the Sacramento River by slicing through basaltic rock and Mossbrae Falls makes a stunning arrival at the river through a wall of moss and ferns. When President George W. Bush came to California to visit Arnold Schwarzenegger this is one of the places the former governor took him to see.

## The Park

Not named for extinct wooly elephants, Mammoth Cave earns its name as the world's longest known cave system with more than 400 miles of passages mapped, so many that the guides like to point out that you could put the second and third longest caves systems inside the limestone labyrinth and have more than 100 miles left over. Human habitation has been traced back as far as 4,000 years and the cave was a commercial center for the production of saltpeter, one of the three ingredients necessary to manufacture gunpowder along with sulphur and charcoal. Protection for the cave arrived in the early decades of the 20th century.

**WHERE/WHEN**

Kentucky/1941

**OFFICIAL POLICY REGARDING DOGS**

Dogs are not allowed in any cave but above ground Mammoth Cave National Park is about as dog-friendly as it gets in the National Park Service.

## What Your Dog Will Miss

Your dog will not see the flash-lights of the tour guides illuminate such fancifully named formations as Grand Avenue, Frozen Niagara and Fat Man's Misery.

# Nearby Places to Hike With Your Dog

No need to leave the park. A variety of leg-stretching hikes less than two miles are available around the Visitor Center, including the *Green River Bluffs Trail* that snakes through thick woods to a promontory above the Green River. It also leads to the Historic Entrance of the cave that is no longer in use except as an exit - for both people and blasts of cold underground air.

For prolonged canine hiking head for the *North Side Trails*. A half-dozen mid-length day hikes launch into the dark hollows and hardwood forests from the *Maple Spring Trailhead* (North Entrance Road). A favorite day hike for your dog here is the 7.9-mile *Good Springs Loop* that rolls past numerous waterfalls. This labyrinth of trails cuts through rugged terrain that has been left in its natural state. In the Big Woods (Little Jordan Road), you can hike the *White Oak Trail* through one of the last remaining old growth forests in Kentucky.

Along Highway 255 (the East Entrance road) is a small parking lot for a short boardwalk trail to Sand Cave. For several weeks in

*A dog can dream - dogs are not allowed to tour Mammoth Cave but the trails along the Green River afford a good look at the Historic Entrance now used as an exit.*

the 1930s, this remote section of woods was the most famous spot in America. A local cave explorer named Floyd Collins became trapped in the cave and the nation became fixated on the rescue efforts that were meticulously detailed in newspapers and radio reports. Rescuers were ultimately unsuccessful in freeing Collins from a leg-pinning rock. The incident spawned books and a movie starring Kirk Douglas, *Ace In The Hole*. The trail stops at a small entrance above Sand Cave so there will not be another repeat performance of the drama.

# MESA VERDE NATIONAL PARK

## The Park

Theodore Roosevelt, spurred on by the tireless campaigning of journalist Virginia McClurg and scores of Women's Clubs, made Mesa Verde a national park to preserve a peerless American archaeological treasure. Mesa Verde ("green table") is a flat-top mountain well over a mile high where the shale and sandstone has been scored into canyons by receding ancient ocean waters. The Anasazi peoples began building adobe dwellings atop the mesa and later in caves and under overhangs in the canyon outcroppings about 1400 years ago. They farmed the area for seven centuries before abandoning their villages for reasons still unknown. The remains of the multi-storied adobe cliff dwellings were stumbled upon by trappers in the 1870s and today there are over 4,700 documented archaeological sites at Mesa Verde.

## What Your Dog Will Miss

Not much hiking-wise; there are no recreational trails in Mesa Verde.

*The Tower House is one of the spectacular relics your dog will miss at Mesa Verde.*

**WHERE/WHEN**
Colorado/1906

**OFFICIAL POLICY REGARDING DOGS**
Dogs are not allowed on any trails or in the archeological sites.
You can walk your dog along the paved roads and she can stay in the campground.

# Nearby Places to Hike With Your Dog

Mesa Verde is the southern anchor for a 233-mile driving loop through southwestern Colorado known as the San Juan Skyway. For much of its route the All-American Road traces the Durango and Silverton Narrow Gauge Railroad and visits old mining towns like Ouray and Telluride and it circles through the San Juan National Forest. The serpentine stretch between Silverton and Ouray got the name "The Million Dollar Highway" because it was so difficult and costly to build although others maintain that it was because of all the gold ore in the rocks that were used for the highway's fill.

The San Juan National Forest, so designated in 1905 as one of America's earliest heritage forests, is loaded with day hikes and back-packing treks through the jagged peaks that earned the area the tag of "America's Switzerland." Many of Colorado's fabled Fourteeners are here - mountains that top out above 14,000 feet. The national forest is divided into three wilderness areas. The most popular and largest - almost the size of Rhode Island - is the Weminuche Wilderness with such popular destinations as the Chicago Basin with views of three Fourteeners and the still-operating railroad that is a national historic landmark. At Lizard Head Wilderness you start hiking with your dog above the treeline at elevations over 10,000 feet as soon as you get out of your vehicle.

*Your dog's hiking in the Lizard Head Wilderness begins above the treeline.*

# MOUNT RAINIER NATIONAL PARK

## The Park

Mount Rainer was selected as the icon to appear on the reverse side of the Washington state quarter. Probably with little debate. The massive 14,410-foot volcano is the highpoint of the Cascade Range that runs up the western spine of the nation and is so prominent it became one of only a handful of national parks designated in the 19th century. The signature mountain is visible for over 100 miles but its summit is often kept shrouded in clouds that produce the "snowiest place on Earth" according to the National Park Service. A boast delivered with the caveat that the only contenders for the honor are places where snowfall is actually measured regularly.

## What Your Dog Will Miss

Jumping on and off the *Wonderland Trail* that circumnavigates Mount Rainier over the course of 93 miles as it trips through wildflower-filled meadows and ascends and descends a steady diet of ridges. The historic trail was built in 1915 and climbs as high as 6,750 feet as it

**WHERE/WHEN**

Washington/1899

**OFFICIAL POLICY REGARDING DOGS**

Dogs are welcome in Mount Rainier National Park - except on trails, off trails, in the wilderness, inside buildings, in amphitheaters or on snow. So basically if you keep your dog's paws in contact with pavement at all times he will be welcome in Mount Rainier National Park.

visits the 25 glaciers covering Mount Rainier. Dogs are permitted to hike on the *Pacific Crest Trail* as it picks its way through the park on its 2,663-mile journey from the Canadian border to the Mexican border.

# Nearby Places to Hike With Your Dog

Approaching from Seattle or Tacoma, just before reaching Mount Rainier National Park you drive through Federation Forest State Park, a swath of 600 acres along the White River of old growth Douglas Firs interspersed with enormous Western Hemlock, Sitka Spruce and Western Red Cedar trees. The paw-friendly twelve miles of trails in the shadow of Mount Rainier are mostly level and easy to trot. Down the *Naches Trail*, an old pioneer footpath, a Gnome Village has sprouted with tiny doors and wee hammocks and even a miniature outhouse that is sure to set your dog's nose to twitching.

The southern entrance to Mount Rainier comes via the White Pass Scenic Byway that rambles 124 miles through "Washington's Volcano Playground." Much of the land that is not in the national park is administered by the Gifford Pinchot National Forest and is dog-friendly. At the White Pass Ski Area you won't even have to leave the Byway (Route 12) to access the *Pacific Crest Trail* and hike 3.5 mostly level miles with your dog to Sand Lake. Packwood Lake is another destination tagged by an easy, low-elevation hike. Glacier Lake requires a bit

*The trees grow large along the White River in western Washington.*

more effort with an elevation gain of 800 feet over two miles but comes with an added bonus of huckleberries along the footpath.

# NORTH CASCADES NATIONAL PARK

## The Park

This is glacier country - the North Cascades is the most heavily glaciated area in the continental United States. The current park glacier census stands at 318 with countless more snowfields that are fed by some of the heaviest snowfalls in the world, between 400 and 700 inches in an average year. The millions of North Cascades acres have been carved up among various federal agencies since 1968 but most of the region - 93% - has been designated as the Stephen Mather Wilderness Area, named after the first director of the National Park Service.

## What Your Dog Will Miss

There are 400 miles of trails that your dog will never see but neither will most day hikers. Backpackers and mountaineers are stalking peaks such as Mount Terror, Mount Despair and Mount Fury but prizes like Cascade Pass and Mount Triumph can be scored on a day hike.

**WHERE/WHEN**
Washington/1968

**OFFICIAL POLICY REGARDING DOGS**
Dogs are not allowed in the national park, period. They can, however, tiptoe through the park on the *Pacific Crest Trail.*

------------------------------------------------------------

# Nearby Places to Hike With Your Dog

Dog owners in the North Cascades head for the tail-friendly Ross Lake National Recreation Area sandwiched between the North Unit and the South Unit of the national park. The only paved access road to the area is Washington State Route 20, the North Cascades Highway,

*The view of Diablo Lake is open to any dog willing to make the hike.*

that runs across the recreation area. Parking areas along the highway are splattered with outings from spirited day hikes to overnight expeditions.

Quick leg stretchers introduce the natural and human history of the mountains at the Visitor Center in the Newhalem Area. The *River Loop* slips through alpine forests to a free-flowing section of the Skagit River. Diablo Lake, with its rich turquoise waters, is the central jewel of the Ross Lake NRA and several canine hiking opportunities exist here. The *Diablo Lake Trail* on the north shore is an out-and-back affair of nearly four miles with just a modest elevation gain. Thunder Creek, that feeds the lake with fine glacial sediment, is shadowed by a 38-mile trail but the first steps are an easy canine hike of less than a mile to a crossing suspension bridge. The popular *Thunder Knob Trail* crawls through dry forest terrain to views of Diablo Lake and surrounding peaks.

More long-distance outings are available upstream at Ross Lake, the largest of the three man-made reservoirs on the Skagit River. *The East Bank Trail* runs 17 non-strenuous miles along the shore of the lake. At Ross Dam a short walk of less than a mile leads down to the 540-foot tall dam and across the road the *Happy Creek Forest Walk* takes a short stroll through an ancient creekside forest.

*It is not complete wilderness in the North Cascades.*

## The Park

By 1898 America consisted of 45 states and most of the Olympic Peninsula had still not even been mapped. When the final geographical mysteries of the contiguous United States, including its westernmost and northwesternmost points, were finally filled in President Theodore Roosevelt wasted no time extending federal protection to the Olympic Peninsula, beginning with its highest peak, Mount Olympus. By the time Roosevelt's fifth cousin Franklin formally signed the Olympic National Park into existence in 1938 it included one million acres and most of the interior of the peninsula. Much of the remainder of northwest Washington is a tapestry of Native American tribal lands, national forests and state parks. Seventy-three miles of rock-studded and sandy Pacific Ocean coastline joined the national park in 1953.

## What Your Dog Will Miss

Your dog can only experience Hurricane Ridge, named for the hellacious winter storms that strafe the mountains, from your vehicle on the paved 18-mile road that reveals the glacier-covered slopes and plunging river valleys of the heart of the Olympic Peninsula. Similarly your dog will not be able to trot among the giants of the Hoh Rain Forest, North America's only temperate rainforest.

**WHERE/WHEN**
Washington/1938

**OFFICIAL POLICY REGARDING DOGS**
Dogs are allowed in campgrounds and picnic areas but can also stretch legs on the short *Peabody Creek Loop* trail at the Park Visitor Center and hike the *Spruce Railroad Trail* that trips along the north shore of Lake Crescent, ringed by sharp mountain peaks and often cited during debates of "the most beautiful lake in America." Dogs are permitted on all the Kalaloch Beaches and a section of Ruby Beach on US 101.

# Nearby Places to Hike With Your Dog

Luckily for trail dogs everywhere the denizens of the rainforest are not restrained by national park boundaries. The Quinault Rain Forest in the adjacent dog-friendly Olympic National Forest has everything the Hoh does except the reputation and the crowds. Best explored on two loop trails off South Shore Road at Lake Quinault, the *Quinault Rain Forest Trail* penetrates an old-growth forest where firs and spruce can tickle 300 feet in height. Clubmoss draping branches and thick canopies suffocate the light on the forest floor of this four-mile canine hike.

In a half-mile loop the *Rain Forest Nature Trail* interprets the creation of this lush arboreal paradise. At one magical turn in the trail you stand with your dog beneath all four titans of the Pacific rain forest - Western red cedar, Sitka spruce, Douglas fir and Western hemlock - growing in a row. This is the result of their

*Olympic National Park beaches make for a challenging hike.*

propagating on the mossy safety of large ancestors fallen on the forest floor. When the nurse logs decay completely their thriving wards are left with a distinctive hollow root pattern.

If this has only whetted your appetite for rain forests you can take the dog on a rough-and-tumble hike on the *Dry Creek Trail #872*. Other routes in the Quinault National Recreation Trail System lead to a cedar bog, waterfalls and along the lakeshore. Lake Quinault bills itself as the "Valley of the Rain Forest Giants" and several short spurs reveal several charter members, including the Worlds' Largest Spruce Tree. This monster soars 191 feet high with a circumference only a few whiskers shy of 59 feet around. On the North Shore a half-mile trail takes you to a gnarled big cedar that is believed to be over 1,000 years old. You can easily stand inside the ancient wonder with your dog.

The rare unspoiled forests of the Olympic National Forest contrast with the second growth timber stands of the Duckabush Recreation Area (22 miles north of Hoodsport). Here the *Interrorem Nature Trail* wanders amidst trees flourishing beside head-high cedar stumps from timber harvesting. The trail is reached via the *Ranger Hole Trail* that descends sharply 100 feet to the lively waters of the Duckabush River.

# PETRIFIED FOREST
# NATIONAL PARK

## The Park

The mineralized remains of an ancient Mesozoic Forest were tens of millions of years in the making but the nation's largest field of petrified wood wasn't formally described until 1851. The Atlantic and Pacific Railroad built though this area in the 1880s, bringing profiteers to the forest. They carried off petrified wood specimens and dynamited the largest logs in search of quartz and purple amethyst crystals. In 1895 the Arizona Territory began petitioning for federal protection and

*Dogs are welcome to trot through the Painted Desert.*

on December 8, 1906 Theodore Roosevelt designated the petrified forest as America's second national monument. In 1962, with the addition of the scenic landscape of the Painted Desert, the Petrified Forest became America's thirty-first national park.

**WHERE/WHEN**
Arizona/1962

**OFFICIAL POLICY REGARDING DOGS**
"Please take your furry friends on trails, even backpacking in the wilderness area."
That is not a misprint. That is straight from the park policy.
Wow.
It does not get any dog-friendlier than that. No dogs allowed in any park buildings but outside all 146 square miles of desert scrub and color-streaked badlands are open to your dog.

## What Your Dog Will Miss
Only the exhibits inside the Visitor Center and the Rainbow Forest Museum.

---------------------------------------------------------------

# Nearby Places to Hike With Your Dog
Right here. Three paved loops - all less than a mile long - lead into the barren desert amidst remains of the petrified forest. Although short and easy to hike, these interpretive trails are completely without shade so have a supply of water ready on hot days. The *Crystal Forest Trail* meanders through the remains of obliterated petrified logs, leaving you to only imagine what these crystalized trees once looked like before the pillaging that led to the creation of the Petrified Forest National Monument. Some of those prehistoric trees can be seen on the *Long Logs* path. Extinct conifers form the largest concentration of petrified wood left in the park.

The *Agate House Trail* leads up a slight rise to a reconstructed Anasazi Indian Pueblo built entirely of colorful petrified wood sealed with mud. Also available to canine hikers is the one-mile *Blue Mesa Trail*. A sharp drop in the path leads to an amphitheater surrounded by banded badlands of bluish clay called bentontite. Rainwater is the brush that creates streaky patterns in the porous hills.

Out in the Painted Desert are 52,000 acres of backcountry to explore with your dog, including dinosaur fossils and over 350 Native American sites. The 2.5-mile hike through the Jasper Forest of colorful petrified wood is one of the easiest, using an old gravel road constructed by the Civilian Conservation Corps back in the 1930s. The Blue Forest is a similar destination with more easy going on an old road grade.

*Finding gardens of prickly pear in the desert always draws interest from trail dogs.*

## The Park

The craggy rock faces and rolling chaparral in central California are the souvenirs of an extinct volcano that was jostled by rumblings in the giant San Andreas Fault. The earthquakes created deep gorges in the landscape and formed talus caves so striking that after homesteader Schuyler Hain arrived in the area in 1891 he became a proselytizer for preserving the massive black and gold monoliths of rock. The unofficial "Father of Pinnacles" led tours and wrote enough letters to government officials to convince President Theodore Roosevelt to set aside 2,500 acres as a national monument in 1908. The Pinnacles were volleyed among different federal agencies until January 2013 when Barack Obama was able to create his first national park.

**WHERE/WHEN**
California/2013

**OFFICIAL POLICY REGARDING DOGS**
Dogs are allowed only in the campground on roads that are paved and in parking lots.

## What Your Dog Will Miss

Dogs are not the only animal actively excluded from enjoying the Pinnacles. Park officials erected about 30 miles of barbed wire fence to keep out feral pigs - a protection measure that has spawned "pig fence hikes." Your dog will also miss treks along the narrow and steep *High Peaks Trail* that are accomplished with toe holds in the rocks and handrails. The best times in the Pinnacles are had by rock climbers and cave adventurers, activities which would preclude dogs anyway.

**Dogs and people stroll Carmel Bay on equal footing.**

# Nearby Places to Hike With Your Dog

Standing between the Pinnacles and the Pacific Ocean only 40 miles away are the Santa Lucia Mountains. While not much more than one mile high the range does feature the steepest coastal elevation in the continental United States. The Santa Lucias are part of the Los Padres National Forest that offers 1,257 miles of maintained, mostly-dog-friendly trails. The mountains are part of the Northern Section of the national forest, lubricated by six major watersheds.

The most popular segment of the Santa Lucias is the Big Sur coastline south of the Monterey Peninsula, a stretch that includes Point Lobos that Australian painter Francis McComas was moved to gush that it was the "greatest meeting of land and water in the world." Your dog won't be able to enjoy that exact spot as dogs are not allowed on any trails in Point Lobos State Reserve. Dogs are also banned from the other state parks at Big Sur but one little sliver of coastal paradise welcomes dogs - Pfeiffer Beach.

A short, sandy trail leads to one of the most beautiful public beaches in California. The sand is wrapped in spectacular rock formations making Pfeiffer Beach a very secluded place

*It doesn't get much better for dogs than at Pfeiffer Beach.*

indeed. The rocks in the surf make exciting play in the waves for dogs. For the less adventurous canine swimmer, a small freshwater stream feeds into the beach. There is also room to hike along the sand to the north for restless canine hikers. And you won't be lacking for canine company at Pfeiffer Beach - most everyone who makes the drive down the long, narrow access road seems to have a dog in the back seat.

To the north on Monterey Peninsula Carmel-by-the-Sea stands as a contender for dog-friendliest town in America. Dogs can run un-leashed on the soft white sand of Carmel City Beach among the craggy headlands that frame Monterey Bay. For real canine hiking, two miles north of town on Highway 68 is Jack's Peak Regional Park. More than 10 miles of sporty trails cover the 525-acre park, including routes to the highest point on the Monterey Peninsula. From the trails you can enjoy spectacular views of both the bay and Carmel Valley. And forget about not being able to hike with your dog in the Pinnacles.

# REDWOOD NATIONAL AND STATE PARKS

## The Park

Sporting bark impervious to insects and having no known diseases, coastal redwoods can live 2,000 years, grow over 350 feet tall and weigh 500 tons. Logging began in 1851 with smaller, more manageable trees but as technology improved bigger and bigger trees were taken. There were two million acres of redwoods when logging began; today about five percent of those lands remain with the planet's tallest trees. In the 1920s, three California state parks were established to protect the redwoods and in 1968 Redwood National Park was ushered into existence to preserve additional groves. Together the parks protect about 40,000 acres of the ancient forest.

## What Your Dog Will Miss

Your dog can accompany you on a drive along State Road 254 through the Avenue of the Giants where you will find the largest stand of old-growth redwoods in the world, highlighted by five of the tallest living trees, including the 370-foot Champion Tree. This road became famous as a tourist attraction for its three "drive-thru" trees,

**WHERE/WHEN**
California/1968

**OFFICIAL POLICY REGARDING DOGS**
Dogs are not allowed on park trails, at ranger-led programs or inside park buildings. Dogs can stay in campgrounds, nosh at picnic sites and patrol parking areas. Dogs are permitted at the following beaches: Crescent, Gold Bluffs, Freshwater and Hidden. Another beach just outside the park to the south that welcomes dogs is Clam Beach.

all of which are still alive. They are privately owned and require a toll. She just won't be able to get out of the car on the drive.

# Nearby Places to Hike With Your Dog

The closest place to get your dog on the trail under majestic redwoods is the Smith River National Recreation Area, located adjacent to Jedediah Smith Redwoods State Park. Established in 1990, the 305,000-acre park features Smith River, the largest Wild & Scenic River System in the United States - more than 300 miles have been so designated. It is the last free-flowing river in California without a dam.

The marquee footpath is the *South Kelsey National Recreation Trail*, the remnants of an historic transportation link between the Pacific Ocean at Crescent City and the gold mines in the Klamath River region. This is a

*Big dog, bigger tree.*

long linear trail that leaves between Horse and Bucks creeks and follows the South Fork of the Smith River for seven miles before beginning an ascent to 5,775-foot Baldy Peak at the 13-mile mark. Campgrounds are available on the route, which continues another 15 miles into Klamath National Forest.

Shorter day hikes with your dog are available throughout the recreation area. A walk of nearly two moderate miles on *Craig's Creek Trail* finds many redwood trees along the South Fork. The *Myrtle Creek Trail* is an interpretive hike along an old mining flume where miner Jim Slinkard once found a 47-ounce gold nugget shaped like an axe. Experienced canine hikers can tackle the *Devil's Punchbowl Trail* where switchbacks climb steeply to two postcard lakes tucked in the mountain peaks.

North of the park, Lake Earl is California's largest lagoon, probably formed 5,000 years ago when expanding sand dunes plugged a shallow depression in the Smith River plain. The Tolowa Indians used the natural resources here and there is evidence of their village life in the park. Twenty miles of canine hiking are scattered throughout this prehistoric sand dune complex that features 11 miles of coastline. Wooded hillside trails and grassy meadows abound but the prime attraction in the Lake Earl State Wildlife Area are the 250 species of birds, including the rare Canada Aleutian goose, that visit the wetlands and lakes here. The *Dead Lake Loop* is the one canine hike to do at Lake Earl if you visit under a time constraint.

# ROCKY MOUNTAIN NATIONAL PARK

## The Park

In the late 1800s when the United States government wanted to encourage settlement of its vast western lands it passed a series of Homestead Acts. An Irish nobleman named Lord Dunraven and his agents began making claims along the Continental Divide in Colorado, not to farm and ranch but to build an estate of several thousand acres to develop into a private hunting reserve for rich huntsmen. His scheme alarmed locals in nearby Denver and ignited passion to preserve the area that eventually led to President Woodrow Wilson signing legislation for Rocky Mountain National Park in 1915.

## What Your Dog Will Miss

When you drive up the Trail Ridge Road on the highest continuous paved road in America above the treelike and beyond an altitude of 12,000 feet your dog will not be able to get out of the vehicle for any of the interpretive trails and there will be no canine hiking at Bear Lake or the signature park mountain, Longs Peak, either.

**WHERE/WHEN**
Colorado/1915

**OFFICIAL POLICY REGARDING DOGS**
Dogs are not allowed on park trails or in the backcountry. Dogs can walk on roads and in parking lots. They can also join you in campgrounds and picnic areas.

------------------------------------------------------------

# Nearby Places to Hike With Your Dog

Fortunately Rocky Mountain National Park does not hold a monopoly on outstanding Colorado peaks. In fact, a couple hours to the south your dog can hike to the summit of the highest mountain in the

Centennial State, Mount Elbert. It is the second highest mountain peak in the Lower 48 and the highest spot in America where your dog is allowed to go. Located in the Sawatch Range of the San Isabel National Forest, the peak was named for Samuel Elbert who was a controversial territorial governor of Colorado in 1873. The first recorded summit was by H.W. Stuckle of the Haydon Survey in 1874. Before that, the

*The Mount Elbert summit is as high as your dog can hike in the U.S.*

more famous Pikes Peak was assumed to be the highest point in Colorado.

Mount Elbert is still not well known, despite its lofty position as the highest peak in the Rocky Mountains. Some members of the "14ers," the group of outdoor enthusiasts who tackle all 53 of Colorado's 14,000-foot mountains, look at Mount Elbert with a degree of scorn because it is so "easy" to summit. There were even people who piled rocks on neighboring Mount Massive to give it the extra twenty feet it would need to surpass Mount Elbert. The summit has been reached by jeep and there have been proposals over the years to build a road to the top of Mount Elbert.

Of course, "easy" is relative and all prudent precautions for being on a 14,440-foot mountain must be taken. But any trail dog accustomed to a ten-mile hike can scale Mount Elbert. There are five routes to the top, the most popular being the *North Mount Elbert Trail*. From the trailhead to the summit is 4.5 miles, the first two climbing through alpine forests. After the trail bursts above the treeline the route switches back twice before pulling straight to the summit. There is no rock scrambling or "mountain climbing" necessary. Views along the way are outstanding and unforgettable when you reach the roof of the Rocky Mountains.

Closer to the park is Arapaho National Recreation Area that is cobbled together around a series of alpine lakes known collectively as the "Great Lakes of Colorado." A four-mile circumnavigation of Monarch Lake serves up views of the mountain valleys and soaring summits of the Indian Peaks Wilderness. The tail-friendly trails of Indian Peaks are some of the most visited wilderness trails in the United States with elevations reaching up to 13,500 feet. East of the town of Estes Park dogs can hike off-leash through Lion Gulch in the Homestead Meadows.

## The Park

Saguaro National Park brackets the city of Tucson with the Tucson Mountain District to the west and the Rincon Mountain District to the east. The stately saguaro cactus, symbol of the American West, was first protected by President Herbert Hoover on March 1, 1933 in one of the last acts he performed before leaving office. There are an estimated 1.6 million saguaro plants in the park. Beyond the statement cacti the park preserves and interprets the history of human settlement in the Sonoran Desert dating to prehistoric times. The desert scrub also gives way to pine-oak woodlands inside the park as the mountains rise to 8,666 feet in elevation.

**WHERE/WHEN**

Arizona/1994

**OFFICIAL POLICY REGARDING DOGS**

Dogs are allowed only on roadways and picnic areas and must not be taken on any trail or off-road.

## What Your Dog Will Miss

The primary attraction of Saguaro National Park is the 8.3-mile driving loop through the Rincon Mountain District and some of the greatest concentrations of America's largest cacti. Your dog will enjoy the ride but won't be able to join in any of the short exploratory walks along the route. And the 150 miles of Sonoran Desert trails are off-limits.

-------------------------------------------------------------

# Nearby Places to Hike With Your Dog

Your dog won't be able to trot among the giant cacti of Saguaro National Park but she can still see the best of the Sonoran Desert in neighboring Tucson Mountain Park. The national park, in fact, was once part of the local park. Originally, 60,000 acres were withdrawn from the Homesteading Act of 1873 to be used as Tucson Mountain

Park. About half was returned for use by World War I veterans and part of that land became Saguaro National Park.

Miles of old desert roads and trails crisscross through boulders, palo verde and ocotillo plants in the park. Some of the best stands of giant saguaro outside the national park can be found on the 5.4-mile out-and-back *David Yetman Trail*, named for a local television host and desert authority. Other long linear trails include the 4.4-mile *Gates Pass*

*Even a small stream can be doggie heaven in the Sonoran Desert.*

*Trail* and the *Star Pass East Trail* along a route to early copper mines. The namesake mountains in the park are more like large hills and most of the canine hiking is easy going on gentle grades. Moonlight hikes are popular in the desert and the park stays open until 10:00 p.m. Come sundown find yourself a hillside to sit with your dog and admire the memorable sunset for which the park is known.

North of Tucson Catalina State Park is a hit-and-miss affair for dogs but the 2.3-mile *Canyon Loop Trail* that visits the differing habitat types found in this beautiful desert terrain. The trail rolls gently up and down through riparian arroyos and past stands of the desert sentinels. The loop winds up with an unexpected hidden stream complete with a delightful doggie swimming hole.

*Sometimes a picnic table is the best your dog will be able to do in a national park.*

# SEQUOIA/KINGS CANYON NATIONAL PARK

## The Park

The wood of the largest tree on earth, the giant sequoia, splinters easily and does not make useful commercial lumber. That did not stop loggers with big dreams from felling thousands of the magnificent trees as soon as it was technologically feasible. So when America came up with the idea for national parks it did not take long for some wily conservationists to maneuver legislation into law in 1890 to protect as many of the remaining sequoia groves as possible. The Giant Forest boasts five of the ten largest trees in the world, including the reigning behemoth by volume - the General Sherman Tree. In the bargain the park also protects a large swath of the Sierra Nevada Mountains, America's longest mountain range.

**WHERE/WHEN**
California/1890

**OFFICIAL POLICY REGARDING DOGS**
Dogs are not permitted on any park trails but can visit the campgrounds and picnic areas.

## What Your Dog Will Miss

Your dog will not be able to meander through the ancient groves of sequoia trees in the Giant Forest. Your dog will not be able to make the easy walk to Topokah Falls. Your dog will not be able to trot up the historic rock steps of Moro Rock, a massive granite landmark in the park. Most disappointingly your dog will not be able to tag the summit of Mt. Whitney, the highest point of the High Sierras and the highest elevation in the continental United States. It is especially frustrating since all but the final ascent to the 14,505-foot summit are open to dogs since the 11-mile *Whitney Portal Trail* begins in the dog-friendly Inyo National Forest. The summit resides in the national park.

# Nearby Places to Hike With Your Dog

Dogs can hike on the shoulders of the national park in Sierra National Forest and Inyo National Forest and to the south in Sequoia National Forest. And there is the opportunity to brush shoulders with some of earth's most mammoth trees. About five miles north of Kings Canyon National Park and the famous General Grant Grove is the Converse Basin Grove where your dog can get up close to a famous giant sequoia, the Boole Tree.

Converse Basin is a giant sequoia graveyard. This area was once quite possibly the finest sequoia grove that ever was. Massive trees over 300 feet high were enthusiastically felled by loggers - often for little more than shingles. One 285-foot sequoia known as the General Noble Tree was cut in 1893 to display at the Columbian Exposition in Chicago and the Chicago Stump can be seen in the forest today. Among the trees destroyed in the

*Felled sequioas are as impressive as living trees.*

Converse Basin was the oldest known giant sequoia to have been cut down - 3200 annual growth rings were counted. So many trees were taken that the area is known as Stump Meadow.

The hiking trail in the Converse Basin is a 2.5-mile loop to reach the Boole Tree. Leading straight out from the parking lot you are quickly on the edge of Kings Canyon with its open, sweeping views as you switchback up the ridge. Shortly after finishing your climb a side trail leads into a depression containing the Boole Tree, once thought to be the largest giant sequoia in the world but more exacting measurements have since placed it eighth. No one knows why this great tree was spared when equally large trees were brought down.

If you have spent the day looking at giant sequoias in the landscaped national parks, your encounter with the Boole Tree might come as a bit of a shock. It is related to its brothers in Kings Canyon National Park like the wolf is to your dog. Surrounded by dense forest growth, it is actually possible to not immediately recognize the Boole Tree from the main trail. But once you see your dog up against its massive trunk - its ground perimeter of 113 feet is the greatest of all giant sequoias - there is no mistaking this special tree.

# SHENANDOAH
# NATIONAL PARK

## The Park

The Blue Ridge Mountains that host Shenandoah National Park are the oldest rocks on earth. A billion years ago these mountains were higher than the Rockies. Time has weathered and rounded the peaks and valleys that we see today. But what we see in Shenandoah has not been left to the hand of nature, as we have come to expect in our national parks. Shenandoah is very much a planned park. Herbert Hoover established a Summer White House on the Rapidan River (the park is only 75 miles from Washington D.C.) helping to trigger wilderness development. During the Great Depression Shenandoah was officially designated a national park and Franklin Roosevelt's "Tree Army" planted hundreds of thousands of trees on slopes that had been cleared for farms and firewood

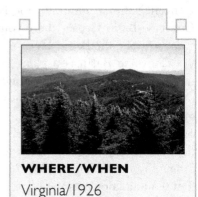

**WHERE/WHEN**

Virginia/1926

**OFFICIAL POLICY REGARDING DOGS**

The only major prohibition regarding dogs in Shenandoah National Park is that they are not allowed to join the fun on Ranger Programs.

in the previous two hundred years. At the same time construction began on the 105-mile Skyline Drive that is today the only public road in Shenandoah National Park.

## What Your Dog Will Miss

Your dog is welcome at just about every stop along the Skyline Drive - only 20 of the more than 500 miles of hiking trails are off-limits for dogs. Those twenty miles often involve awkward passages and rock climbs that would be difficult for a dog to navigate. One such trail that can not be on your favorite trail companion's "to-do" list is on Old Rag Mountain, a climb so fine that it is considered by many to be the best hike on the East Coast. But generally your dog will be able to visit the postcard views and waterfalls in Shenandoah National Park.

---------------------------------------------------------------

# Nearby Places to Hike With Your Dog

The Skyline Drive links to the 469-mile Blue Ridge Parkway at its southern end, as tail-friendly as Shenandoah National Park. The Parkway is its most popular destination in the National Park System - receiving more than 19 million recreation visits per year. Dogs are allowed on the more than 100 varied trails down the length of the Blue Ridge Parkway, ranging from easy valley strolls to demanding mountain summit hikes. In the winter, when the Parkway closes at higher elevations, hiking with your dog right down the two-lane road is a special joy.

Just northeast of the park is Sky Meadows, a jewel in the Virginia state park system. The real star here is the meadows - there simply aren't many open air hikes available across Northern Virginia. The trail system offers about ten miles of marked paths that can be molded into canine hiking loops, the most popular being the North Ridge-South Ridge circuit. The *South Ridge Trail* utilizes an old farm road while the *North Ridge Trail* sashays its way up the mountain like a traditional hiking trail. You are probably best served by going up the South Ridge since it is not as steep and the views are longer coming down the North side.

For those looking for a full day of hiking with your dog at Sky Meadows the *Appalachian Trail* is 1.7 miles away and there are loop options up there as well. If you just want to enjoy the meadows you can confine your explorations to the *Piedmont Overlook Trail* on the North Ridge. It is also possible to enjoy the park without hard climbing on the *Snowden Trail* interpretive nature walk and the *Shearman's Mill Trail*.

Taking a hiking break on a trademark Skyline Drive stone wall.

# THEODORE ROOSEVELT NATIONAL PARK

## The Park

Theodore Roosevelt first came to the Dakota Territory in the fall of 1883 to hunt bison and became besotted with what he called the "perfect freedom of the West." A year later he returned to rebuild his spiritual life after his wife and mother passed away on the same day. Roosevelt became a rancher, part-time sheriff and full-time booster of the rugged landscape and a strenuous life which he championed in three books about his experience.

Theodore Roosevelt National Park in the Little Missouri Badlands was established by Harry Truman in 1947 as the only memorial national park the United States ever developed. Roosevelt's Elkhorn Ranch is preserved in the park and accessed by gravel roads. Most of the park is grasslands interrupted by coulees and broken buttes that caused migrating pioneers to call this "the badlands" because it was no place to get a wagon across. Wildlife spotting of bighorn sheep, bison and wild horses is the prime attraction of the park which is split into two units, north and south of the gateway town of Medora.

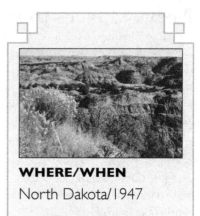

**WHERE/WHEN**
North Dakota/1947

**OFFICIAL POLICY REGARDING DOGS**
Dogs are not permitted in park buildings, on trails or in the backcountry.

*There is nothing like the national grasslands for a good doggie roll.*

## What Your Dog Will Miss

About 100 miles of foot trails, including nature walks to such attractions as Caprock Coulee, Painted Canyon and Prairie Dog Town. Your dog will also not be able to complete the celebrated 96-mile *Maah Daah Hey Trail* (the name comes from the local Mandan Indian term for "an area that has been around for a long time.") that punctuates the badlands while connecting the units of the national park.

------------------------------------------------------------

# Nearby Places to Hike With Your Dog

Theodore Roosevelt National Park is enveloped by more than one million acres of the Little Missouri National Grasslands, the largest grassland in the country. Here your trail dog will find much of the same experiences as those missed out in the park itself. The *Maah Daah Hey* and its side trails play a leading role but be prepared for full days of canine hiking.

The *Cottonwood Trail Loop* delivers a canyon-like experience through groves of cedar and aspen during its 15-mile exploration. The *Long X Trail* traces the bottomlands of the Little Missouri River and uses the grasslands to close its 11-mile loop. The Badlands become very real on the four-mile *Summit Trail* that connects the *Maah Daah Hey* to the Summit Campground. Only well-behaved and tightly-controlled dogs should venture onto the ledge trails cut into the coulees with 200-foot drop-offs.

*Your dog is king of all he can survey on the national grasslands.*

# WIND CAVE NATIONAL PARK

## The Park

Wind Cave was discovered in 1881 when brothers Jesse and Tom Bingham heard a whistling sound in the ground and Tom's hat was blown off by a small hole when they went to investigate. As the cave was explored it was probed for mineral wealth and then exploited for tourism. Those commercial efforts ended in 1903 when Theodore Roosevelt made Wind Cave America's first cave protected as a national park. Subsequent explorations have uncovered more than 100 miles of underground passages making Wind Cave the sixth longest known cave system in the world.

## What Your Dog Will Miss

The cave tours, mostly, but you were never expecting to take your dog on those in the first place. You also won't be able to complete the 111-mile *Centennial Trail* that was developed in 1989 as a monument to South Dakota statehood with your dog. That trail, broken into 22 walkable chunks by strategically developed trailheads, runs through the national park.

------------------------------

**WHERE/WHEN**
South Dakota/1903

**OFFICIAL POLICY REGARDING DOGS**
Above ground are more than 30 miles of trails through one of the last remaining intact prairies int he country but canine hiking can be had on only two short trails, each about one mile in length. *Elk Mountain Trail* is a sporty loop around the campground that traverses the beautiful prairiescape with expansive views.
A second option for your dog is the *Prairie Vista Trail* surrounding the Visitor Center. The park's third nature trail, *Rankin Ridge*, is a no-doggie-go.

# Nearby Places to Hike With Your Dog

Right next door to Wind Cave National Park is the largest state park in America outside Alaska, Custer State Park. Your dog will still find endless prairies to hike through here - the park is famous for its free-ranging bison herd that grazes about a quarter of the park's 73,000 acres. The 3-mile hillside *Prairie Trail* off the Wildlife Loop Road is a rolling loop that explodes into a spectacular wildflower display in the summer.

As the park transitions to the dark-hued spruce trees that gave the Black Hills their name take your dog to Badger Hole, home to Badger Clark, South Dakota's first poet-laureate. Clark planned part of the footpath behind his four-room cabin that picks its way along rocky hillsides displaying mixed spruce and hardwoods.

The marquee hikes in Custer State Park congregate around Sylvan Lake, a calendar-worthy pool of water flanked by giant granite boulders that formed when Theodore Reder dammed Sunday Gulch in 1921. A pleasant one-mile loop circumnavigates the lake and offers plenty of dog-paddling along the way. Hardy canine

*Dog paddling around Sylvan Lake makes for a perfect doggie day.*

hikers will want to make a detour to the demanding *Sunday Gulch Trail* that passes over massive boulders and along splendid walls of lightly shaded granite.

*The dog's-eye view from the highest point east of the Rocky Mountains.*

Sylvan Lake is also a popular jumping off point to climb Harney Peak, at 7,242 feet the highest point in the United States east of the Rocky Mountains. The most traveled route to the summit is on *Trail 9*, a 6-mile round trip. There is some rock scrambling near the top but your dog can make it all the way and even go up the steps into the observation tower.

# WRANGLE-ST. ELIAS NATIONAL PARK

## The Park

With more than 13 million acres under management and another nine million acres of wilderness, this is the largest park in the National Park Service. The closest of Alaska's six national parks to the Lower 48, the Wrangell-St. Elias National Park is defined by its list of superlatives aside from its size. The greatest concentration of glaciers in North America is here; about one-quarter of the park is under ice. The Nabesna Glacier is 75 miles long and the longest valley glacier in the world. The St. Elias Mountain Range is the highest coastal range in the world; Mount St. Elias is the second highest mountain in the United States at 18,008 feet. The

**WHERE/WHEN**
Alaska/1980

**OFFICIAL POLICY REGARDING DOGS**
Dogs are allowed on all the park trails AND in the backcountry.

other namesake mountain range, the Wrangell Mountains, is a volcanic field and Mount Wrangell is Alaska's highest and largest volcano. Its last eruption was in 1900 and it can often be seen belching steam on clear, cold days.

## What Your Dog Will Miss

Anywhere you want to go in Wrangell-St. Elias National Park your dog can go too. Of course, when your annual visitation (less than 100,000) is about the same as the number of people who visit Great Smoky Mountains National Park on a long weekend you can exercise a little lighter grip on the rule book.

------------------------------------------------------------

# Nearby Places to Hike With Your Dog

While you can find a few day hikes near the Copper Center Visitor Center most of the hiking in Wrangell-St. Elias National Park is of the backpacking variety and often without trails. Only two gravel roads penetrate this vast wilderness for a total of about 100 miles. If you

navigate the 59-mile Mc-Carthy Road to the Kennicott Visitor Center it is a two-mile hike to the toe of Root Glacier for your dog to sample walking on a glacier; another two miles accesses the Erie Mine where copper was extracted until 1938. You can also get to the Toe of the Kennicott Glacier on a day hike with your dog from the Kennecott Mill Town - an ideal way to experience Alaskan wilderness without disappearing for a week.

*A dog can get tired hiking through 13 million acres of parkland.*

*When trails are found in Wrangle-St. Elias National Park they are likely to be empty.*

# YELLOWSTONE NATIONAL PARK

## The Park

It was not until 1869 that the first expedition - privately funded - to chronicle the wonders of the Yellowstone River was launched. Before that only bits and pieces of information had trickled from the wilderness to the outside world. What David Folsom, Charles Cook and William Peterson reported led to an official government expedition the following year and within three years the wonders of Yellowstone had inspired the concept for a "national park."

Today three million people sample the more than 350 waterfalls and 500 distinguished geysers. Half of all the world's mud pots and boiling springs and geo-thermal features are inside the park. Yellowstone Lake is the largest high-altitude body of water on the continent and the big mammal wildlife viewing is the best you will find on any American vacation - the bison herd is the country's largest and oldest.

**WHERE/WHEN**
Wyoming/1872

**OFFICIAL POLICY REGARDING DOGS**
Dogs are prohibited from all trails and boardwalks. Dogs can stay in campgrounds but are not allowed more than 100 feet from any roads.

## What Your Dog Will Miss

If you bring your dog to Yellowstone hoping to see famous landmarks like Yellowstone Falls, the Grand Canyon of Yellowstone, Old Faithful geyser and mud pots you are in luck. The park is laid out so that all the signature attractions are a short stroll from parking lots where you can leave your dog comfortably in your vehicle and still see. If you bring your dog to Yellowstone hoping to experience the majesty of the backcountry without the crowds you are completely out of luck.

# Nearby Places to Hike With Your Dog

Three of the five entrances to Yellowstone National Park are covered by the Gallatin National Forest. Established by President William McKinley in 1899, Gallatin's 1.8 million acres contain six mountain ranges that share the restless geology of its famous neighbor - on August 17, 1959, at 23 minutes before midnight, two massive blocks of the earth's crust dropped 10 feet tilting lakes, dropping houses into giant sinkholes and triggering a landslide that buried 19 campers.

Any type of canine hike can be sculpted on the more than 2,000 miles of trails in the Gallatin National Forest. Hard by the Northeast Entrance to the park is the Clarks Fork Picnic Area, developed on the site of a wooden water flume that was built a century ago to deliver water to a now-collapsed power plant. Beyond the historic ruins *Russel Creek Trail #3* leads into the Absaroka-Beartooth Wilderness and some of the most rugged mountain hiking America has to offer.

*Hiking along the Yellowstone River - outside the national park.*

The East Gate is the province of the Shoshone National Forest and the Buffalo Bill Cody Scenic Byway. Before automobiles, when Teddy Roosevelt was riding horses he called this route from the town of Cody to the park along the North Fork of the Shoshone River "the most scenic 50 miles in the world." There are more than 1,300 miles of trails in the five wilderness areas that cross three mountain ranges. One of the most popular trailheads near Yellowstone is the *Fishhawk Trailhead.*

A short distance from the East Gate on the byway is a roadside memorial to 15 firefighters who lost their lives in a battle against a Blackwater wildfire in 1937. A six-mile National Recreation Trail leads up to the site of the catastrophe and gains nearly 4,000 feet in elevation to the site of the one-time Forest Service lookout tower that no longer exists. Sites where the men were trapped are marked by bronze and stone memorials built by fellow Civilian Conservation Corps members and hauled up the mountain by stock.

# YOSEMITE NATIONAL PARK

## The Park

Federal protection in the Yosemite Valley of the High Sierra predates the national park concept - Abraham Lincoln signed the Yosemite Grant in 1864 setting aside the massive cinnamon-colored trees of the Mariposa Grove "for the pleasuring of the people." By the 1870s there were three stagecoach roads built to the park and homesteaders were still constructing cabins until finally in 1890 Yosemite was afforded national park status. Today Yosemite is the size of Rhode Island and its familiar granite cliffs and waterfalls and drive-through trees have provided many poster shots for the National Park Service.

## What Your Dog Will Miss

There won't be any rock climbing on El Capitan for your dog. There won't be any hiking to the three tiers of Yosemite Falls, the sixth highest waterfall in the world. There will not be any trotting through the three groves of ancient giant sequoias in the park. There won't be any adventures in the high country meadows for your dog.

------------------------------

**WHERE/WHEN**
California/1890

**OFFICIAL POLICY REGARDING DOGS**
Dogs are not allowed on the 800 miles of park trails, save for the 3.5-mile trail at the *Wawona Meadow Loop*. Hey, they built a golf course in one of Yosemite's largest meadows so dogs should at least be able to walk around the edges.
Dogs are also allowed to hike around the Yosemite Valley which is not nothing with the Merced River and its famous high-plunging waterfalls. But if you can't score a parking spot in the valley dogs can not ride in on shuttle buses.

# Nearby Places to Hike With Your Dog

Your dog can't get on the trail through the famous Mariposa Grove that started the park but he can walk among giant sequoias five miles south of Yosemite in the Nelder Grove. Naturalist John Muir discovered this stand of redwoods in 1875 and as he investigated he happened upon a retired miner named John Nelder who was homesteading there. The area was heavily logged thereafter, mostly sugar pines, firs and cedar and the largest sequoias still stand.

The *Shadow of the Giants Trail*, now a National Recreational Trail, was built in 1965. The self-guiding interpretive path meanders for about

**Dogs can hike along the Yosemite Valley floor and enjoy a swim in the Merced River.**

a mile through the Nelder Grove, one of eight growing above the Kings River. Unlike sequoias in national parks, the 100 giants here remain in dense forest and you can walk right up to the largest trees. Those would be Old Granddad and the Kids, a grouping of giant sequoias on a ridgeline and Bull Buck, one of the world's five largest arboreal monarchs. After a half-mile hike from the lower campground you meet Bull Buck, nearly 250 feet tall, 99 feet around at the base and probably 2700 years old.

The Yosemite High Country is tackled by the Tioga Road, Highway 120, culminating in Tioga Pass at the park's entrance. Tioga Pass is California's highest automobile pass at 9.945 feet. Just outside Yosemite is a 3/4-mile nature trail around a glacial lake called the *Nunatak Trail*, or "Island of Life." If your dog is itching to get on a trail after a visit to Yosemite this is a refreshing leg-stretcher. Beyond that are two million acres of the Inyo Forest and dead ahead is the odd Mono Lake, saltier than the seven seas and home to organisms found only there. The Mono Basin National Scenic Area was the first place in the country so designated by the park system.

# ZION NATIONAL PARK

## The Park

Father Silvestre Veles de Escalante, an adventurous Spanish priest searching for an overland route to California, was the first to describe the topography of southern Utah in 1776. Within a generation the Old Spanish Trail was busy moving settlers through these canyons and mountains. After Brigham Young arrived in 1850 he sent emissaries here who saw the handiwork of nature at the junction of the Colorado Plateau, Great Basin and Mojave Desert and named it "Kolob" as the heavenly place nearest the residence of God. John K. Hillers, a government photographer, recorded dramatic images of Zion Canyon in the early 1870s and Frederick Samuel Dellenbaugh painted canvases of the canyon that were put on display at the 1904 World's Fair in St. Louis. William Howard Taft designated the far reaches of southwestern Utah a national monument in 1909 but unless you carried the job title of "explorer" the pictures and paintings were the only ways anyone knew about Zion Canyon until 1917 when old wagon roads were paved over and touring cars could reach the varietal sandstone canyons, massive mesas and endless rock towers. Even today only one road accesses the granddaddy of Utah's National Parks, used by almost three million visitors each year - so many that shuttle buses are required in the spring and summer to reach the heart of the park in Zion Canyon.

**WHERE/WHEN**
Utah/1919

**OFFICIAL POLICY REGARDING DOGS**
Dogs are not permitted on any park trails (except the uninspiring *Pa'rus Trail* out of the South Campground along the Virgin River), in public buildings, in the wilderness area or on the shuttle buses. Dogs can stay in the campground and visit the picnic areas.

### What Your Dog Will Miss

Some of the National Park Service's best adventure hikes including the ascent to Angel's Landing through all 21 of Walter's Wiggles, the discovering of Hidden Canyon, standing beneath Weeping Rock and the water-walking in the Virgin River through the Zion Narrows. Your dog will also not get on the trail to see the world's second largest arch - Kolob Arch.

-----------------------------------------------------------

# Nearby Places to Hike With Your Dog

The same iron oxides and minerals that produce Utah's "Color Country" in Zion National Park are responsible for Coral Pink Sand Dunes State Park. The winds are pinched in the highlands so much they can't sustain enough speed to carry away the grains of eroded Navajo sandstone that have piled up in a notch in the mountains for thousands of years. A quick introduction to dune formation comes on a 1/2-mile nature trail at the day-use lot. The *Two Dunes Trail* visits a wind-blown barchan (crescent-shaped dune) and a star-shaped dune caused by winds coming from several directions before returning in less than two miles.

*The Dixie National Forest stands in admirably for Zion.*

The Dixie National Forest spreads out to the west of Zion National Park with more than 100 miles of trails between the outpost towns of St. George and Cedar City. The marquee canine hike is the *Whipple Trail*, designated a National Recreation Trail. The full trail is eight miles long with plenty of ups and downs for flavor as it climbs to big views of Zion National Park. Except in early summer after snow melts don't expect much water time for your dog in the meadows and Engelmann spruce forests along the way. At Navajo Lake dog owners will find that watery recreation and the *Pinks Trail* and the *Virgin Rim Trail*, with views of the river that cuts the great Zion canyon. The *Pinks Trail* is a healthy half-mile climb that rewards canine climbers with pink limestone cliffs and a stand of gnarled and ancient bristlecone pine tucked into scattered stands of aspen and Douglas fir.

## Other Books On Hiking With Your Dog from Cruden Bay Books
### www.hikewithyourdog.com

DOGGIN' AMERICA: 100 Ideas For Great Vacations To Take With Your Dog - $19.95
DOGGIN' THE MID-ATLANTIC: 400 Tail-Friendly Parks To Hike With Your Dog In New Jersey,
Pennsylvania, Delaware, Maryland and Northern Virginia - $18.95
DOGGIN' CLEVELAND: The 50 Best Places To Hike With Your Dog In Northeast Ohio - $12.95
DOGGIN' PITTSBURGH: The 50 Best Places To Hike With Your Dog In Southeast Pennsylvania - $12.95
DOGGIN' ORLANDO: The 30 Best Places To Hike With Your Dog in Central Florida - $9.95
DOGGIN' ASHEVILLE: The 50 Best Places To Hike With Your Dog In The Carolina Blue Ridge - $12.95
DOGGIN' NORTHWEST FLORIDA: The 50 Best Places To Hike With Your Dog In The Panhandle - $12.95
DOGGIN' ATLANTA: The 50 Best Places To Hike With Your Dog in North Georgia - $12.95
DOGGIN' THE POCONOS: The 33 Best Places To Hike With Your Dog In Pennsylvania's Northeast
Mountains - $9.95
DOGGIN' THE BERKSHIRES: The 33 Best Places To Hike With Your Dog In Western Massachusetts
- $9.95
DOGGIN' NORTHERN VIRGINIA: The 50 Best Places To Hike With Your Dog In NOVA - $9.95
DOGGIN' DELAWARE: The 40 Best Places To Hike With Your Dog In The First State - $9.95
DOGGIN' MARYLAND: The 100 Best Places To Hike With Your Dog In The Free State - $12.95
DOGGIN' JERSEY: The 100 Best Places To Hike With Your Dog In The Garden State - $12.95
DOGGIN' RHODE ISLAND: The 25 Best Places To Hike With Your Dog In The Ocean State - $7.95
DOGGIN' MASSACHUSETTS: The 100 Best Places To Hike With Your Dog in the Bay State - $12.95
DOGGIN' CONNECTICUT: The 57 Best Places To Hike With Your Dog In The Nutmeg State - $12.95
DOGGIN' THE FINGER LAKES: The 50 Best Places To Hike With Your Dog - $12.95
DOGGIN' LONG ISLAND: The 30 Best Places To Hike With Your Dog In New York's Playground - $9.95
DOGGIN' THE TIDEWATER: The 33 Best Places To Hike With Your Dog from the Northern Neck to
Virginia Beach - $9.95
DOGGIN' THE CAROLINA COASTS: The 50 Best Places To Hike With Your Dog Along
The North Carolina And South Carolina Shores - $11.95
DOGGIN' AMERICA'S BEACHES: A Traveler's Guide To Dog-Friendly Beaches - $12.95
THE CANINE HIKER'S BIBLE - $19.95
A Bark In The Park: The 55 Best Places To Hike With Your Dog In The Philadelphia Region - $12.95
A Bark In The Park: The 50 Best Places To Hike With Your Dog In The Baltimore Region - $12.95
A Bark In The Park: The 37 Best Places To Hike With Your Dog In Pennsylvania Dutch Country - $9.95

CPSIA information can be obtained
at www.ICGtesting.com
Printed in the USA
LVHW081706240521
688343LV00012B/2137